Threads of Revelation

PILLAR OF FIRE
TOWARDS THE PROMISED LAND

———————

PAT DENIM

Reviews are important to independent authors, so if you have the time, I would really appreciate you leaving one for this book. Thank you.

Pat Denim

Threads of Revelation

PILLAR OF FIRE:
Towards the Promised Land

Cover Design by: Scatterling Design

Paperback: ISBN 978-1-962097-02-4
Ebook : ISBN 978-1-962097-03-1

LCCN : 2023945053

Table of Contents

Sands Of Liberation   10
The Midwives' Rebellion   13
The River's Embrace   14
The Voice Of I Am   16
Reluctant Messenger   18
Bitter Demands   20
Crumbling Lives   21
River Of Death   23
Footsteps Of Ancestors   25
River Of Blood   27
Days Of Darkness   29
Omen Of Anguish   31
Marked With Blood   33
Midnight's Cry   36
Pillars Of Cloud And Fire   38
Swallowed By The Waters   40
A Song Of Deliverance   42
Tambourine Dance   45
Wilderness Of Sin   48
Lightened Burden   50
Fearful Encounter   52
Humanity's Laws   54
The Value Of Life   55
Scrolls Of Justice   58
Hands Of Wickedness   60
The Mount Of Revelation   63
The Divine Blueprint   65

A Sacred Dwelling Place 67

A Place Of Offering 69

Garments Of Glory 71

Passing On The Mantle 74

Consecrating The Sanctuary 76

Gifted Hands 78

Shattering The Tablets 80

Land Of Dreams 82

Frightful Revelation 84

Bezalel's Masterwork 86

Oholiab's Artistry 88

Ark Of The Covenant 90

A Sanctuary's Splendor 92

Robes Of Purple And Bells 95

Following A Cloud 97

Blood Is Shed 100

Aroma Of Devotion 102

Offerings At The Door 103

Guilt Erased 105

Sin's Price Paid 107

Fragrance Of Forgiveness 109

The Significance Of Blood 111

Anointing Oil And Blood 114

Fire From Above 117

Devoured By Fire 119

Dietary Restrictions 121

The Unclean Mother 123

Alone 125

Flight Of The Bird 128

In The Face Of Flow 130

Fate Of The Goat   134
Forbidden Secrets   136
Forbidden Acts   138
Fair Judgments, Just Measures   140
Pure Gifts   142
Sacred Times   145
Cursing God's Name   148
Fair Transactions   150
Exile And Despair   154
Just Compensation   156
Offering By Fire   159
Appointed Times   161
Forgotten Inheritance   164

SANDS OF LIBERATION

In ancient Egypt, a tale unfolds,
Among those yearning to break Egypt's hold.
Was Raised in Pharaoh's court, a child unknown,
His destiny to rise, his power to own.

His childhood shrouded, purpose unclear,
Yet God's hand guided, ever near.
A burning bush called, a divine decree,
He confronted Pharaoh, "Set my people free!"

Staff in hand, he faced the throne,
Demanded freedom, the battle unknown,
Pharaoh angered, plagues ensued,
A divine spectacle, the land imbued.

From blood to frogs, gnats, and flies,
To hailstorms raging through the skies,
Egyptian firstborns to meet their fate,
While Israelite's prepared, they could not wait.

Passover night, a sacred hour,
Lamb's blood marked doors from Gods power,
The Angel of Death passed by their door,
Israelite's set forth, their nation to restore.

With haste they fled, their journey begun,
Through desert vast, under scorching sun.
Onward they ventured, a desert expanse,
Trusting in God, a divine dance.

The Red Sea parted, by their guide,
Egyptian pursuers swallowed by the tide,
In the wilderness they trod, though tired,
Divine provisions, their needs supplied.

Manna and quail, bestowed each day,
They followed the pillar, a tenuous way.
At Sinai's peak, midst thunder and smoke,
A covenant embraced, their destiny woke,

So hear this tale of Exodus bold,
Of liberation, faith, and stories retold,
From Moses' early years to triumph's sight,
A timeless saga of strength and might.

So, journey with them, embrace the past,
Unveil the lessons that eternally last,
The epic of Exodus, forever renowned,
A tale of liberation, on hallowed ground.

Explore the realm where priests hold sacred sway,
Unveiling the path to redemption, come what may.
With offerings and sacrifices, sins atone,
A journey of purity, to the Lord's throne.

From burnt offerings' smoke that ascends on high,
To the scapegoat, bearing sins, a solemn cry.
For in Leviticus, each detail is defined,
A blueprint for holiness, where faith aligns.

The purity codes, intricate and precise,
Reveal divine wisdom, beyond mortal eyes.
From clean and unclean, to dietary decree,
The Israelites' lives transformed, eternally.

Behold the festivals, marked with joyful cheer,
Passover, Pentecost, and the Day of Atonement near.
With reverence, the chosen ones gather and sing,
A symphony of devotion, a heavenly offering.

Yet Leviticus extends beyond laws and rights,
A call to justice, compassion shining bright.
To care for the widow, the orphan, the poor,
To love thy neighbor, as the Lord did before.

Unlock Leviticus, a timeless treasure,
Boundless wisdom, a sacred measure.
Immerse in its pages, insights profound,
A journey to the divine, to be found.

THE MIDWIVES' REBELLION

Israel's sons embarked for Egypt's shore,
With households assembled, ready to explore.
Reuben, Simeon, Levi, and Judah grand,
Issachar, Zebulun, and Benjamin's band.

Seventy people descended from Jacob's seed,
But Joseph was already in Egypt to lead.
Joseph died, with his generation,
But Israel's sons increased, a growing sensation.

A new king arose, who didn't know Joseph's fame,
He feared Israel's people, too mighty to tame.
He ordered taskmasters to oppress them with labor,
But Israel's numbers grew, and they did not waver.

Midwives were told to slay newborn boys,
Yet they defied, preserving life's joys.
God blessed them for their fearful bravery,
And Israel's people became more mighty.

Pharaoh commanded to throw sons in the Nile,
But daughters were allowed to live for a while.
Thus, Exodus 1 tells of Israel's rise,
How God protected them from Pharaoh's lies.

THE RIVER'S EMBRACE

In Levi's house a man was wed,
And from their love a son was bred.
But fearing harm, his mother did hide,
The child away for three months' tide.

Amidst the papyrus reed, a basket made,
With tar and pitch, its form well-laid,
She hid the child among the reeds' shade,
By Nile's bank, where none would invade.

From afar, the sister's watchful eyes,
Observed what fate would soon arise,
Pharaoh's daughter, with much surprise,
Found the child, tears filled her eyes.

With pity, she took him as her own,
Realizing his heritage was known,
The sister, quick to seize the chance,
Suggested calling their mother's hence.

So the child was nursed with care
And Pharaoh's daughter paid her share.
She named the boy "Moses," for he was saved,
From the waters where he'd been laid.

Years later, Moses saw the strife,
Of his fellow Hebrews' hard life,
And witnessed an Egyptian's beating hand,
Upon a man from his own land.

Looking left and right to see,
No one around, he struck and killed the enemy,
But when he saw two Hebrews fight,
He asked why they caused such a sight.

But they challenged his authority,
And accused him of a murderous atrocity,
So Moses fled from Pharaoh's hand,
And in Midian, settled in a foreign land.

There, he helped the priest's daughters draw water,
And saved them from the shepherds' slaughter,
And in turn, he was given a wife,
Zipporah, she was the love of his life.

Their son was named Gershom in a foreign land,
For Moses was a stranger, far from home's sand.
And as time passed, the Israelites groaned,
In bondage, their pain and sorrow moaned.

But God remembered His covenant true,
With Abraham, Isaac, and Jacob too.
He saw their plight and took notice,
And heard their cry for help with focus.

THE VOICE OF I AM

Moses watched the flock on Jethro's land,
In the wilderness, a desolate strand,
He led them to Horeb, the mountain of God,
Where an angel's appearance made him applaud.

From a burning bush, a fire did blaze,
Yet was not consumed, it left him amazed,
Moses drew near, a sight so surreal,
The voice of God spoke, and Moses did kneel.

"I am the God of Abraham, Isaac, and Jacob," said He,
"Remove your sandals, for holy ground you see.
My people suffer oppression and pain,
I have come to rescue, a new land to gain."

God spoke to Moses, gave him a task,
To lead His people out of Egypt at last,
But Moses doubted, "Who am I to lead?"
God promised to help, signs to succeed.

Moses went forth to his people, he said,
"The God of your fathers has sent me ahead."
"What is His name?" they asked with a stir,
God replied, "I AM WHO I AM, forever."

Moses and the elders of Israel he gathered,
To the king of Egypt, their message delivered,
But the king refused, his heart so cold,
So God sent plagues, the story we're told.

With miracles and wonders, Egypt was struck,
The king relented, the people were unstuck,
Favored in the sight of the Egyptians, they went,
With plundered gold and silver, they were sent.

RELUCTANT MESSENGER

"What if they will not believe me?" he said,
Or hear the words that I have said?
"They'll say, 'The LORD has not appeared,
To you, his message we won't heed.'"

"What's in your hand?" the LORD replied,
"A staff," Moses said, full of pride.
"Throw it upon the ground," He said,
And when he did, it turned to dread.

A serpent writhed upon the floor,
Moses fled, he could take no more.
"Reach out your hand and grasp its tail,"
The LORD commanded, without fail.

Moses did as he was told,
And it transformed back to old.
"So they may believe," the LORD did say,
"That I have appeared to you this day."

The LORD said, "Put your hand inside
The fold of your robe," and Moses tried.
When he took it out, it was leprous white,
But then restored, to his delight.

"If they won't believe these signs so true,
Then water from the Nile will do.
Pour it on the dry ground bare,
And blood shall flow, a sign so rare."

Moses replied, "I'm slow of speech,
And not at all eloquent, I preach."
But the LORD said, "I'll be with your mouth,
And teach you what to say, there's no doubt."

BITTER DEMANDS

"Please send someone else," Moses said,
And the LORD was angry, it was said.
"Aaron the Levite is your kin,
He speaks fluently, he'll help you win."

"You'll put the words in his mouth, and then
I'll instruct you both again and again.
He'll speak to the people, he'll be your voice,
And you'll be God to him, he'll have no choice."

Moses went to his father-in-law Jethro,
And said, "Let me go, I must go.
See if my brothers are alive and well,
And if they're not, then it's farewell."

The LORD said, "Go back to Egypt now,
And perform the wonders I've shown you how.
But Pharaoh's heart I'll harden tight,
And he won't let the people out of sight."

CRUMBLING LIVES

In Egypt's land of slavery,
Moses and Aaron came to plea,
"Let my people go," they said,
"To celebrate with God ahead."

Pharaoh scoffed at their request,
"Who is this Lord?" he expressed,
"I will not let Israel depart,
And neglect their work to start."

But Moses and Aaron did insist,
God's wrath would come if they resist,
"Just three days' journey, let us go,
To sacrifice and honor Him so."

Pharaoh's anger grew each day,
He ordered more work and less hay,
No straw to make the bricks they need,
The labor grew heavier, indeed.

The foremen cried out in dismay,
Their people beaten day by day,
"Why do you treat us this way?
We cannot meet the quota, we say."

Pharaoh accused them of being lazy,
Their request to go was seen as crazy,
The foremen saw they were in trouble,
Their people's lives now just rubble.

Moses and Aaron faced their ire,
Feeling the weight of Pharaoh's fire,
"Why did you make us repulsive so?
To put a sword in the enemy's hold."

Moses prayed to the Lord on high,
"Why have You brought harm and strife?
Pharaoh has done harm to Your people,
Please rescue them from his evil."

RIVER OF DEATH

.Moses and Aaron came to plea,
"Let my people go," they said,
"To celebrate with God ahead."

Pharaoh scoffed at their request,
"Who is this Lord?" he expressed,
"I will not let Israel depart,
And neglect their work to start."

But Moses and Aaron did insist,
God's wrath would come if they resist,
"Just three days' journey, let us go,
To sacrifice and honor Him so."

Pharaoh's anger grew each day,
He ordered more work and less hay,
No straw to make the bricks they need,
The labor grew heavier, indeed.

The foremen cried out in dismay,
Their people beaten day by day,
"Why do you treat us this way?
We cannot meet the quota, we say."

Pharaoh accused them of being lazy,
Their request to go was seen as crazy,
The foremen saw they were in trouble,
Their people's lives now just rubble.

Moses and Aaron faced their ire,
Feeling the weight of Pharaoh's fire,
"Why did you make us repulsive so?
To put a sword in the enemy's hold."

Moses prayed to the Lord on high,
"Why have You brought harm and strife?
Pharaoh has done harm to Your people,
Please rescue them from his evil."

FOOTSTEPS OF ANCESTORS

God spoke to Moses, saying with power,
"I'll show Pharaoh in his darkest hour,
He'll let my people go, under duress,
And drive them out of his land, with distress."

"I am the LORD, known to Abraham,
Isaac, and Jacob, but by another name.
I made a covenant, gave them Canaan's land,
And heard their cries, in Egypt's cruel hand."

"I'll bring you out of slavery's chains,
Redeem you with judgment and great pains,
Make you My people, and be your God,
Lead you to the land where your fathers trod."

But the Israelites, in their despair,
Did not listen, too burdened to care.
God commanded Moses and Aaron to go,
To free the Israelites from their foe.

The sons of Reuben, Simeon, and Levi,
With their families, were named to thrive,
The heads of their households, by name,
God called Moses and Aaron, with the same.

God spoke to Moses, saying again,
To tell Pharaoh, let My people go, amen.
But Moses doubted, unskilled in speech,
God assured him, His power would reach.

RIVER OF BLOOD

Moses and Aaron, sent by God,
To Pharaoh they were called.
"Let my people go," they said,
But Pharaoh's heart was hard and cold.

God knew what would come to pass,
He'd harden Pharaoh's heart.
But through His signs and wonders,
The Egyptians would soon depart.

Aaron's staff became a serpent,
The wise men did the same.
But Aaron's swallowed theirs up,
Proving God's power and name.

Then came the Nile, turned to blood,
And all the fish did die.
The Egyptians couldn't drink a drop,
Their wells had all run dry.

But Pharaoh's heart remained the same,
Hardened, stubborn, blind.
He didn't care for Egypt's fate,
Nor the people left behind.

Seven days passed with no relief,
The people dug for water.
God's power had been clearly shown,
But Pharaoh's heart got harder.

DAYS OF DARKNESS

The LORD spoke to Moses,
"Go to Pharaoh," He said,
"And tell him, 'Let My people go,
So they may serve Me instead.'"

"If you refuse," the LORD warned,
"Frogs will cover all your land,
In your house and on your bed,
Even in your pots and pans."

Moses told Aaron to stretch his staff,
And so the frogs did come,
But Pharaoh's priests did the same,
So the frogs were not undone.

Pharaoh begged for mercy,
And Moses asked when he'd like relief,
"Tomorrow," Pharaoh said,
And Moses asked for his belief.

The next day, the frogs were gone,
But Pharaoh's heart was hard,
So the LORD sent a plague of gnats,
On man and beast, yard by yard.

The priests tried to stop it,
But they could not succeed,
And they told Pharaoh, "This is God's work,"
But his heart would not concede.

The LORD spoke to Moses again,
And said, "Tell Pharaoh this,
If he won't let My people go,
Then swarms of flies will fill his house."

But Goshen, where the Israelites lived,
Would be free from the flies' invasion,
So Pharaoh would know that God was there,
Making a clear separation.

Pharaoh said, "You can sacrifice,
But don't go too far away,"
So Moses prayed for the flies to leave,
And Pharaoh promised to obey.

OMEN OF ANGUISH

In Egypt's land, where Hebrews toiled,
The Lord spoke out to Moses, bold,
"Go forth to Pharaoh, let him know,
That I have said, 'Let my people go.'"

But Pharaoh's heart was hard as stone,
And so the Lord made His power known,
With plagues and pestilence, He smote,
The livestock first, but still no vote.

Then boils broke out on all the land,
The priests could hardly take a stand,
But still, Pharaoh would not bend,
His heart was hard until the end.

The Lord then spoke to Moses, "Go,
And tell Pharaoh, it's time to show,
My power, and let my people free,
So all the world will know of me."

Hail came next, so fierce and strong,
The like of which had not been long,
Destroyed the crops and trees alike,
But in Goshen, no hail did strike.

Pharaoh then said, "I confess,
The Lord is righteous, I am less,
I'll let you go, just make it cease."
But Moses knew he lacked true peace.

For Pharaoh's heart was still not right,
He did not fear the Lord's great might,
And so the plagues would still go on,
Until the day he'd see his wrong.

MARKED WITH BLOOD

The Lord spoke to Moses and said,
"Go to Pharaoh, for I have led
His heart astray, and those around
So I may perform wonders renowned.

You'll tell your son and grandson too
How I mocked the Egyptians and slew
Their power, and by my hand
Performed my signs throughout the land.

So Moses and Aaron came
To Pharaoh, and this they did proclaim:
"Let my people go," the Lord commands,
"So they may serve me in all the lands.

Refuse, and tomorrow you'll see
Locusts that will cover all you'll see.
They'll eat the rest of what's left to you,
And every tree in the field will they chew.

Your homes, your servants', and Egypt's all,
Will be filled with locusts, in a swarm so tall.
Something unseen since the start of time,
Until this very day of yours and mine."

PAT DENIM

Pharaoh's servants spoke and said,
"How long shall this man be a snare to our stead?
Let the people go, and let them serve
The Lord their God, or all will curve."

Pharaoh then asked, "Who shall go,
To serve the Lord, and what will they show?"
Moses said, "All will come with me,
Our young and old, our flocks and family.

We must hold a feast to the Lord,
And with His blessings, we will be adored."
Pharaoh warned, "Watch out for evil,
On your mind, don't be so medieval."

Moses pleaded, "Not just the men alone,
But every soul in our household, bone by bone."
So, Pharaoh let them go at last,
But the Lord hardened his heart, and trouble was cast.

The Lord then commanded Moses to reach
His hand out over the land to teach
The locusts to come and eat away
Every plant, and leave no green that day.

The locusts came in such great numbers,
Darkness fell over the land and encumbers
Egypt, and they could not see
For three days of total misery.

34

Pharaoh let them go, but said,
"Leave your flocks and herds behind, instead."
Moses replied, "No, we must have
Sacrifices and burnt offerings, we crave.

We will take our livestock with us too,
To serve the Lord our God, and to renew
Our faith, until we reach the place
Where we shall serve Him face to face."

But Pharaoh's heart was hardened still,
And he refused to bend his will.
"Be gone!" he said, "Do not come back again,
Or you'll see my face in vain."

MIDNIGHT'S CRY

The Lord spoke to Moses with a command,
One final plague on Egypt's land,
Pharaoh will release you, this is true,
And when he does, he'll drive you through.

Tell the people to ask their neighbors,
For silver and gold, as they'll be givers,
And the Lord gave favor to his nation,
Even Moses held high estimation.

At midnight, the Lord will go out,
And the firstborn will scream and shout,
From Pharaoh's throne to the lowly slave,
Even cattle will meet their grave.

A great cry will be heard all around,
In Egypt's land, the wailing sound,
But the sons of Israel will be safe,
Protected by the Lord's saving grace.

Pharaoh's servants will come and bow,
And beg the people to leave now,
But stubborn Pharaoh will not comply,
The Lord will show wonders and multiply.

Despite all the wonders and miracles,
Pharaoh's heart was hardened, it's pitiful,
And the sons of Israel still remain,
In Egypt's land, with freedom to gain.

PILLARS OF CLOUD AND FIRE

The Lord spoke to Moses, saying,
"Sanctify every firstborn to Me,
Be it of people or animals, it belongs to Me."

Moses said to the people,
"Remember this day you departed from slavery,
With a powerful hand, the Lord set you free.
No yeast shall be eaten, it's a day of purity."

On this day, in the month of Abib,
You are about to leave, in a joyous trip.
To the land of milk and honey, promised by the Lord,
Where you shall perform this rite, in one accord.

For seven days, eat unleavened bread,
On the seventh day, a feast to the Lord, be led.
No yeast shall be seen, throughout your borders,
Reminding of the Lord's power, for your sons and daughters.

Tell your son, "It is because of what the Lord did for me,
When I came out of Egypt, I was set free."
Let this be a sign on your hand, on your forehead,
The law of the Lord in your mouth, forevermore stored.

When you reach the land of the Canaanite,
Firstborn of a womb, devote to the Lord, in His sight.
The males belong to the Lord, let this be known,
Firstborn of a donkey, redeem with a lamb, or break its bone.

When your son asks you, "What is this?"
Say, "With power, the Lord set us free, from slavery's abyss.
Pharaoh was stubborn, and the Lord put to death,
Every firstborn in Egypt, humans, animal's their last breath."

Let this sign be on your hand, phylacteries on your forehead,
With a powerful hand, the Lord led you out of Egypt's dread.
When Pharaoh let the people go,
God led them not by the Philistines land , but to and fro.

Lest they change their minds, and return to slavery,
To the Red Sea, he led them, with bravery.
Moses took the bones of Joseph, with the solemn oath,
"God will take care of you, carry my bones with you both."

The Lord went before them, in a pillar of cloud by day,
And a pillar of fire by night, to guide their way.
He did not take them away from the presence of the people,
For with a powerful hand, the Lord leads His people.

SWALLOWED BY THE WATERS

The Lord spoke to Moses, saying,
"Tell the sons of Israel to turn back and camp,
In front of Pi-hahiroth, between Migdol and the sea,
Opposite Baal-zephon, by the sea."

Pharaoh will say they're wandering aimlessly,
"The wilderness has shut them in," he'll believe.
"I will harden Pharaoh's heart," the Lord declared,
"He will chase after them and be ensnared."

Pharaoh and his army took six hundred chariots,
The Lord hardened his heart, and they chased the Israelites,
As they went out boldly, they saw the approaching army,
Fear took over, and they cried out to the Almighty.

"Why have you brought us here to die, Moses"
"We would have served the Egyptians in peaceful doses."
Moses told them not to fear, see the salvation of the Lord,
"He will fight for you; keep silent and trust in His word."

The Lord instructed Moses to lift his staff,
And stretch his hand out over the sea with a laugh,
The waters parted with a strong east wind,
Dry land appeared, and the Israelites grinned.

The Egyptians followed, and the Lord caused confusion,
Chariot wheels swerved, they'd difficulty with their delusion.
The Lord told Moses to stretch his hand again,
The waters swallowed the Egyptians' chariots and men.

The Lord saved Israel from the Egyptians' hand,
The waters were a wall to them, as they crossed dry land.
The Lord was honored through Pharaoh and his army,
And the Egyptians knew that He was Almighty.

A SONG OF DELIVERANCE

Moses and the Israelites,
Sang a song of great delight,
To the Lord, their God above,
For His strength and endless love.

He hurled Pharaoh's horse and rider,
Into the sea with righteous fire,
And saved His people from their plight,
Through His power and His might.

The Lord is a warrior, His name so grand,
He throws His enemies into the sand,
Pharaoh's army drowned in the sea,
His officers lost, unable to flee.

The waters covered them like a stone,
And they sank down, never to roam,
The Lord's right hand so strong and true,
Destroys His foes, there's nothing new.

In His excellence, He overthrows,
All those who rise up and oppose,
His burning anger consumes like chaff,
And His power is a force to be had.

At the blast of His nostrils, waters stood,
The depths congealed, as He surely would,
The enemy said, "I will pursue,
I will overtake and divide the spoils too."

But the Lord blew His wind, and they sank,
Like lead in the mighty waters, no rank,
No one compares to the Lord so great,
Majestic in holiness, who works wonders with His fate.

His right hand reached out to save,
And the earth swallowed the enemy with a wave,
In His faithfulness, He led His people redeemed,
Guided them with strength, to His habitation esteemed.

'
The people heard, and they trembled with fear,
Anguish gripped them, no hope was near,
Even the chiefs of Edom were terrified,
The leaders of Moab trembled and cried.

All the inhabitants of Canaan despaired,
Terror and dread fell, and they were impaired,
But the Lord's arm made them motionless as stone,
Until His people passed over, safe to their home.

He will plant them in the mountain of His inheritance,
Sanctuary established with His hands, for all to reverence,
The Lord shall reign forever and evermore,
And all His people will forever adore.

Miriam, the prophetess, took the tambourine,
And all the women followed, in unison so keen,
They danced and sang to the Lord on high,
For He had saved them, and made them free to fly.

Moses led them from the Red Sea,
Into the wilderness of Shur, so free,
But for three days, they found no water,
And Marah's waters were bitter, no fodder.

The people grumbled at Moses, so dire,
"What are we to drink?" they asked with fire,
But Moses cried out to the Lord in prayer,
And He showed him a tree, with love so fair.

He threw it into the waters, and they became sweet,
A miracle from the Lord, so neat,
And there He made a statute and regulation,
Testing His people, with His divine inclination.

"If you listen carefully to my voice," He said,
"And do what is right in my sight instead,
And keep my commandments and statutes true,
I will put no diseases on you, it's true.

For I am the Lord, your healer and your guide,
And in my grace, you will safely abide."
Then they came to Elim, with water so clean,
And seventy date palms, a sight to be seen.

TAMBOURINE DANCE

Moses and the children of Israel
Sang a song of praise and zeal
To the Lord, their God above,
For His power and His love.

The Lord is their strength and song,
Their salvation all day long,
Their God, their Father, their King,
To Him they lift their voices and sing.

The Lord is a warrior, strong and true,
His name above all names, it's true.
Pharaoh's army, he did defeat,
In the Red Sea, they met their defeat.

The waters covered them like a stone,
Their arrogance and pride were overthrown.
The Lord's right hand, majestic and great,
Destroyed their enemy and sealed their fate.

In His excellence, the Lord overthrows,
Those who rise up against Him and oppose.
His anger burns like a consuming fire,
Reducing His foes to chaff and mire.

At the blast of His nostrils, the waters stood,
Piled up high, like a heap of wood.
The depths of the sea, congealed and still,
The Lord's power and might, His people do fill.

The enemy said, "We will pursue and destroy,
We will divide the spoils and bring them to joy."
But the Lord blew with His wind, strong and free,
And the enemy sank in the mighty sea.

Who is like the Lord, among all gods?
Majestic in holiness, working wonders and odds.
With His right hand, He reached out and saved,
His people from destruction and the enemy's grave.

In His faithfulness, He led them to their home,
In His strength, He guided them to their throne.
All the peoples tremble and despair,
For the Lord, their God, is truly rare.

He will plant His people in the mountain of His love,
His dwelling place, established by His hands above.
The Lord shall reign forever and evermore,
And His people will worship and adore.

Miriam, the prophetess, took the tambourine,
And led the women in dancing and singing.
"Sing to the Lord, for He is highly exalted,
The horse and his rider, He has hurled into the sea."

Moses led the people from the Red Sea's shore,
Into the wilderness, where they thirsted for more.
For three days, they wandered, finding no water,
But the Lord provided, like a caring father.

At Marah, the waters were bitter and undrinkable,
But the Lord showed Moses a tree, remarkable.
He threw it into the waters, and they became sweet,
A testament to the Lord's power, complete.

He made a statute and regulation for His people,
Testing their faith and obedience, like a steeple.
"If you listen and do what is right," He said,
"I will heal you, and no disease will come, instead."

At Elim, they camped beside the waters so fair,
Twelve springs and seventy date palms, beyond compare.
The Lord had provided for His people, once more,
A promise of His love and care, forevermore.

WILDERNESS OF SIN

A journey through the wilderness,
A people without bread or meat,
Their stomachs grumbled with distress,
Their hope and faith, facing defeat.

Moses and Aaron bore the brunt,
Of Israel's discontented cry,
Their complaints, too much to confront,
As they looked up to the sky.

But the Lord above, so kind and true,
He saw their hunger and their pain,
And promised them bread, fresh as dew,
To sustain them through the desert's terrain.

With each day's journey came new trials,
The test of faith and endurance,
Yet the Lord, with love and wiles,
Provided them manna in abundance.

On the sixth day, with twice the portion,
And on the seventh, a day of rest,
Their faith was tested, a new emotion,
But in the end, the Lord's plan was best.

For in the wilderness of Sin,
The people of Israel learned,
That with faith and trust in Him,
Their needs would always be adjourned.

So they called the bread "manna",
A sweet taste of wafers and honey,
A symbol of the Lord's great plan,
To provide for His people, forever sunny.

LIGHTENED BURDEN

Jethro heard the news, far and wide,
Of all that God had done, with pride,
For Moses and the Israelites,
How they were freed from Egypt's sights.

He took in Moses' wife and sons,
And journeyed with them as one,
To meet with Moses in the wild,
At the mountain where God smiled.

They embraced and caught up on life,
And Moses shared his tale of strife,
Of all the hardship they'd endured,
And how the Lord had kept them secured.

Jethro praised the Lord on high,
For saving them from Pharaoh's eye,
He knew the Lord was greater still,
And could thwart the gods' own will.

He offered burnt offerings and feast,
With Aaron and the elders, a feast,
And the next day, he had a word,
For Moses, who judged like a bird.

"Why do you sit and judge alone?
From morn till night, with people prone,
You'll wear yourself out and your crew,
This task is too much for just you."

And so Jethro gave his advice,
To help Moses make a sacrifice,
To choose able men who feared God,
And lead in groups, with an even nod.

They would judge the people each day,
And bring the major matters his way,
But the minor ones they'd handle too,
To ease the burden, for all anew.

Moses listened and obeyed,
And thus the leaders were made,
To judge the people with care,
And Moses could breathe, without despair.

Jethro then bid his farewell,
To Moses, his daughter and sons as well,
And returned to his own land,
Leaving them in God's own hand.

FEARFUL ENCOUNTER

In the third month of their freedom flight
Israelites reached a wilderness site
Sinai's mountain loomed ahead
A place where God's voice would be said

Moses climbed up to speak with the Lord
Who gave him a message to be explored
"Obey my voice and keep my covenant true
You will be my people, chosen and new"

The elders were told and the people replied
"We will do all that the Lord has prescribed"
Moses went back to the Lord with their vow
Who promised to visit them with His power

The people were told to cleanse and prepare
For the third day when God would be there
Boundaries were set for their own protection
Or else they faced the Lord's divine correction

Thunder and lightning filled the morning sky
A trumpet blared and the people trembled high
Moses led them to meet with their God
At the foot of the mountain, they stood in awe

Mount Sinai smoked and quaked with force
God descended on it with fiery source
Moses was called up to the top of the mount
To hear God's message, his faith to recount

The people were warned to stay away
Priests were told to consecrate and pray
Moses and Aaron went up and down
Sharing the Lord's message to all around.

HUMANITY'S LAWS

God spoke the words, clear and true
From Egypt's land, He brought you through
No other gods before Me, He said
Nor idols made, to be worshiped and fed

Remember the Sabbath, keep it holy
For six days work, but on the seventh, solely
Rest and praise the Lord your God
Who made the earth, the sea, the stars above

Honor your parents, don't take a life
Commit no adultery, nor steal, nor lie
Covet not your neighbor's goods or wife
Or anything that belongs to his life

The people saw the lightning flash
Heard the trumpet, the thunder crash
Trembling, they said to Moses, speak for us
Lest we perish in the presence of God's just

Moses reassured, fear not, my friends
God tests us so sinning ends
Stay away from the thick darkness, near God's throne
Obey His words, and blessings will be shown.

THE VALUE OF LIFE

These are the laws that you must set,
To keep order and avoid debt.
If you buy a slave, a Hebrew man,
He'll serve six years, then be free again.

If the slave has a wife by his side,
She'll leave with him, free to abide.
But if his master gave him a wife,
She and their children, for him, are a life.

If the slave wants to stay forever,
His master will make the bond, never
to be broken, pierce his ear with care,
He'll serve for life, his love to declare.

Now if a man sells his daughter away,
A female slave, she cannot go free one day.
If she's displeasing, her master must see,
To let her be redeemed, and her set free.

If her master designated her for himself,
Then he cannot sell her to someone else.
But if he assigns her to be a wife,
She'll have the same rights as a daughter in life.

If he takes another wife for himself,
The slave woman's rights cannot be shelved.
If he does not provide what he should,
She'll go free, without money, she could.

If someone kills another person,
He'll be put to death, it's certain.
If it wasn't planned and was God's will,
Then a safe haven, we'll provide still.

But if he cunningly plans the act,
He must be punished for this wicked pact.
And one who strikes his mother or father,
Shall be put to death, it's no bother.

Kidnappers shall surely be put to death,
And those who strike a slave to their last breath.
If a slave survives a day or two,
No punishment, for he belongs to you.

If a pregnant woman is hit by chance,
And her baby is born before the circumstance,
The guilty shall pay a fine and more,
As the judges decide, he shall not ignore.

If someone destroys a slave's eye,
He shall be set free, and that's no lie.
And if a tooth is knocked out, you'll see,
The slave shall go free, and that's the decree.

If an ox gores a woman or a man,
The owner shall be stoned, and that's the plan.
If warned but doesn't confine the beast,
His life, as well, shall be deceased.

If a ransom is demanded for his life,
He must pay whatever the cost, no strife.
And if the ox gores a son or daughter,
The same rule shall be followed, without any bother.

If the ox gores a male or female slave,
Thirty shekels of silver, the owner must give.
If someone digs a pit and doesn't cover it right,
And an animal falls in, the owner must make it right.

If someone's ox kills another's ox,
They shall sell the live ox, without any shocks.
Divide the proceeds, then all shall be fair,
These laws, for all, must be handled with care.

SCROLLS OF JUSTICE

Laws of old, written in scrolls,
Of theft and fire, and borrowed souls.
An ox or sheep, if stolen away,
Must be repaid, the price to pay.

If caught in act, the thief must pay,
But if at sunrise, guilt will stay.
Restitution must be made,
Or sold if nothing can be paid.

If what was stolen still remains,
Double the price, the thief sustains.
Fields and vineyards, not to graze,
Or restitution will be raised.

If fire spreads, to grain and thorn,
The one who started, must be warned.
Money and goods, to keep in care,
Stolen away, the thief will bear.

If not caught, the owner's hand,
Must be examined by the land.
Breaches of trust, paid in double,
Before the judges, the case to juggle.

Animals borrowed, if harmed or dead,
Full restitution must be fed.
Seducing a virgin, a dowry paid,
Or money equal, if father's aid is swayed.

Sorceress and beasts, must be put to death,
Sacrificing to other gods, takes your last breath.
No oppression, to strangers or kin,
Or widows and orphans, a holy sin.

Lend to the poor, no interest charged,
A pledge returned, before the sun's discharge.
No cursing God, or ruler of men,
Offerings given, to the Lord again.

Be holy, the Lord has said,
No flesh torn, to dogs to be fed.
These laws of old, still hold true,
A guide for us, to live anew.

HANDS OF WICKEDNESS

Do not bear false witness, be true
Do not join hands with wicked few
Do not follow the crowd in sin
Nor join them to pervert justice, within

Do not favor the poor in dispute
Return your enemy's wandering brute
If his donkey falls helpless to ground
Help him lift the load, don't leave it unbound

Do not pervert justice for the needy
False charge and killing, wicked and seedy
Bribes are blindness, don't take that path
Subverting the cause of the just, in aftermath

Do not oppress a stranger in your land
Remember, too, when you were in quicksand
Sow your land for six, let it rest in seven
So the needy may eat, as God has given

Work six days, rest on the seventh
Let the ox and donkey take a leaven
Be careful with all that you do
Don't mention the name of other gods, it's true

Celebrate three feasts in a year
Unleavened bread and harvest, have no fear
All males shall appear before the Lord God
No one shall come empty-handed, as is the nod

No leavened bread for sacrifice, in the night
The fat of the feast, not until morning light
Bring your choice first fruits to God's house
Do not boil a young goat in its mother's souse

God will send an angel before you on your way
Be attentive and obey, do not stray
For God's name is in him, rebellion won't be pardoned
But if you obey, your enemies will be gone

The Amorites, Hittites, and others, God will destroy
Do not serve their gods or do as they employ
Overthrow them, break their stones in pieces
Serve the Lord God, and blessings will never cease

God will remove sickness, and none will miscarry
No one will be unable to have children, it will tarry
God's terror will throw all people into confusion
Enemies will turn their backs, without exception

Hornets will drive out Hivites, Canaanites, Hittites
God won't drive them out in a year, lest the land desolates
Little by little, you will take possession of the land
From the Red Sea to the Euphrates, it will be at hand

Make no covenant with them, nor their gods
Lest they make you sin, with their frauds
Do not let them live in your land
Serve only God, lest it be a snare, unplanned.

THE MOUNT OF REVELATION

Amidst the mount, Moses heard a voice,
"Come up to the Lord," he was called, with choice.
With Aaron, Nadab, Abihu, and elders so wise,
He approached the Lord, to worship with his eyes.

But only Moses could draw near,
Others must keep their distance with fear.
Then he came back to the people with grace,
Reporting the Lord's words and all the laws in place.

With one voice, the people proclaimed their loyalty,
"We'll do all that the Lord commands with great royalty."
Moses wrote down every single word,
Built an altar with twelve stones, his work unblurred.

Young men offered burnt offerings, peace offerings too,
Moses took blood, sprinkled some on the altar, it's true.
The rest in basins, he kept for the next,
Reading the Book of the Covenant, with all due respect.

The people agreed to do all that was told,
Sprinkling of blood, a covenant to behold.
Moses and the elders went up to the mount,
God of Israel showed up, so mighty and grand.

His feet stood on sapphire, clear as the sky,
His hand, merciful, spared the nobles, no lie.
They ate, they drank, and they saw God,
A moment so sacred, it's worth an applaud.

Moses was called to stay on the mount,
To receive the tablets, as the Lord would recount.
Joshua followed, as his servant, to assist,
While Aaron and Hur stayed with the rest of the list.

Moses went up, and the cloud covered the mount,
The glory of the Lord settled, such a paramount.
For six days, the cloud covered the sight,
On the seventh day, the Lord called out with might.

The glory of the Lord was like a consuming fire,
To the eyes of Israel, it was a divine desire.
Moses went up to the mountain's peak,
For forty days and forty nights, with God to speak.

THE DIVINE BLUEPRINT

The Lord spoke to Moses,
"Tell Israel to contribute for Me.
Take from those with willing hearts,
gold, silver, bronze, and works of art.

Violet, purple, and scarlet thread,
fine linen and goat hair for the spread,
Rams' skins dyed red and leather fine,
Acacia wood and oil for light divine.

Balsam oil for anointing and sweet scent,
Onyx and setting stones for ornament,
Build a sanctuary for Me to dwell,
According to the pattern I shall tell.

Make an ark of acacia wood,
Covered in gold, a masterpiece good.
With four gold rings and poles to hold,
The testimony which I will unfold.

An atoning cover of pure gold,
With two cherubim, their wings unfold,
Facing each other on the cover they stand,
Where I will speak with Moses, My command.

A table of acacia wood, pure and bright,
With gold border and dishes just right,
For the bread of the Presence to be,
Before Me, always there to see.

A lampstand of pure gold, a shining light,
With cups, bulbs, and flowers shining bright.
Six branches, three on each side,
With almonds and bulbs, it's a sight to abide.

Thus, the Lord spoke to Moses with care,
And the sanctuary was built, a beautiful lair.
With the ark, table, and lampstand in place,
God dwelled among them, a divine embrace.

A SACRED DWELLING PLACE

The Tabernacle, made with care,
Of fine twisted linen and colors rare,
Violet, purple, and scarlet hue,
With cherubim embroidered through.

Each curtain shall be twenty-eight
Cubits long and four cubits great,
With the same size for all to share,
Five in one group, five in another pair.

On the edge of the outermost curtain,
Loops of violet, fifty for certain,
And fifty more on the other side,
With clasps of gold, the curtains are tied.

Goats' hair curtains shall be made,
Eleven of them, all the same grade,
Thirty cubits long and four wide,
Joined in two groups with six on one side.

Fifty loops on the edge shall be,
Joined with clasps of bronze, so three
Groups of curtains shall be a tent,
A covering of rams' skins, and fine leather bent.

The boards of acacia wood, upright and tall,
Ten cubits long and one and a half wide in all,
Two tenons on each to fit together tight,
Twenty for the south, and twenty for the north, right.

For the back, six boards are due,
And two for the corners, that's true,
Double and complete up to the top,
To form the two corners, with no stop.

Bars of acacia wood shall be made,
Five for each side, and five for the shade,
In the center, one shall pass through,
With gold rings and holders for bars so true.

And lastly, a veil of colors three,
Violet, purple, and scarlet shall be,
Hung on four pillars of acacia with gold,

A PLACE OF OFFERING

Craftsmanship divine, precise and neat,
The altar of acacia wood to complete,
Five cubits long, and five cubits wide,
A square altar, three cubits high to abide.

Horns on four corners, one with the piece,
Bronze overlay, its beauty to increase,
Pails for ashes, shovels, basins and more,
Utensils of bronze, for the altar to store.

A grating of bronze, netting so strong,
Four rings at corners, where it belongs,
Under the ledge, halfway up high,
The netting shall stay, the altar to beautify.

Carrying poles of acacia wood,
Bronze overlay, as it was understood,
Inserted in rings, on two sides it will lay,
Hollow with planks, as it was shown to obey.

In the courtyard of the Tabernacle,
On the south side, hangings so tactile,
Fine twisted linen, hundred cubits long,
Twenty pillars, with bases of bronze so strong.

For the north side, likewise in length,
A hundred cubits, with pillars of strength,
West side with hangings of fifty cubits long,
Ten pillars and bases, its beauty to prolong.

East side, the same, fifty cubits wide,
On one side of the gate, fifteen cubits to abide,
Three pillars and bases, for it to stand,
On the other side, same beauty so grand.

For the gate of the courtyard, a curtain so fine,
Twenty cubits long, woven in a design,
Of violet, purple, and scarlet material so rare,
Fine twisted linen, with four pillars to share.

All pillars around, joined with silver so bright,
Hooks and bases of bronze, shining with light,
A hundred cubits long, and fifty in width,
Five cubits high, with linen so crisp.

All utensils of bronze, for the Tabernacle to hold,
All pegs, of bronze, for the courtyard to unfold,
Clear oil of beaten olives, for the light so grand,
A lamp to burn continually, on their command.

Aaron and his sons, to keep it in order so true,
Before the LORD, from evening to morning anew,
A permanent statute, for the sons of Israel,
Generations to come, the light to excel.

GARMENTS OF GLORY

Summon Aaron, your brother true,
With his sons, a priestly crew.
Chosen from the Israelite kin,
To serve Me, their sacred kin.

Adorn Aaron with garments bright,
Of glory and beauty, a wondrous sight.
Speak to the skilled with wisdom's flow,
Craft his vestments, let them show.

A breastplate, ephod, and robe so fine,
A checkered tunic, a turban divine,
With a sash to complete the attire,
For Aaron and his sons to inspire.

Gold, violet, purple, and scarlet hue,
Fine linen woven, skilled and true.
Embroidered artistry shall abound,
In the ephod's beauty, it shall be found.

Shoulder pieces with bands entwined,
Memorial stones, a treasure defined.
Engrave the sons of Israel's birth,
In onyx stones, a tale of worth.

Filigree gold, delicate and rare,
Adorned with stones, a weight to bear.
As Aaron serves, the stones shall glow,
A reminder of Israel's sacred flow.

Golden settings and chains refined,
Like twisted cords, in pure gold entwined.
On the breastpiece, justice shall rest,
A skilled embroiderer's fine request.

Ruby, topaz, emerald, and more,
Gems arranged, twelve tribes to adore.
Engraved with names, a symbol grand,
On Aaron's breast, a sacred band.

Golden rings on the breastplate's end,
Cords of gold, their purpose to attend.
To the ephod's shoulder, they shall be bound,
In unity, their strength renowned.

Rings of gold on the ephod's side,
With violet cord, securely tied.
The breastplate's bond, unyielding, true,
A symbol of judgment, ever in view.

Aaron, with the breastplate adorned,
Names of Israel's sons, his heart adorned.
Before the Lord, in holy embrace,
A memorial eternal, a hallowed space.

Urim and Thummim, within shall reside,
Guiding Aaron, as he does decide.
When he enters the Lord's sacred place,
Wise judgment he carries, with heavenly grace.

In poetic verse, this tale is told,
Of garments crafted, precious and bold.
Aaron and his sons, a chosen few,
To serve Me faithfully, in all they do.

PASSING ON THE MANTLE

In fine wheat flour, unleavened and pure,
Make bread and cakes, wafers to secure.
One bull and two rams without blemish sought,
With unleavened bread in a basket brought.

Present them all to the tent's entrance,
Aaron and his sons washed with water hence.
Garments donned, turban on the head,
Holy crown on the turban placed and spread.

Anointing oil on his head to pour,
And on his sons, tunics to explore.
Sashes to wrap, caps to fit,
A permanent statute, priesthood to commit.

The bull then slaughtered before the Lord,
Blood on the altar's horns poured and stored.
All the fat that covers entrails and liver,
Burnt on the altar to deliver.

The ram's blood sprinkled around the place,
Cut into pieces, washed with grace.
Burnt on the altar as a soothing aroma,
Offered by fire, a holy diploma.

The other ram's blood on Aaron's ear,
His sons' ears, thumbs, toes with no fear.
The altar's blood and oil combined,
Sprinkled on all, with consecration aligned.

Fat and bread in Aaron and his sons' hands,
Waved as an offering, the Lord demands.
The breast of Aaron's ram to consecrate,
Consecrated as their portion, truly great.

The holy garments of Aaron's kin,
Shall be passed on after him within.
Boil the ram's flesh for the priests' food,
A consecration, holy and good.

CONSECRATING THE SANCTUARY

A sacred place for God to meet,
An altar of acacia wood complete,
One cubit wide and long, two high,
With horns of gold reaching towards the sky.

The sides, the top, the horns, all pure,
A gold molding added to secure,
Two gold rings on opposite sides,
For poles of wood to hold and provide.

Place it in front of the veil,
Near the ark where God prevails,
Aaron shall burn incense there,
Every morning and evening with great care.

Only pure incense shall be used,
No strange or burnt offering infused,
Once a year atonement to be made,
With blood of the sin offering to be paid.

For every son of Israel counted,
A half-shekel contribution mounted,
To make atonement for each one,
Rich and poor paying the same sum.

A basin of bronze for washing too,
For Aaron and his sons to renew,
Wash their hands and feet with water,
So they can minister without falter.

The finest spices to be taken,
Liquid myrrh, cinnamon, and fragrant cane,
Cassia and olive oil too,
A holy anointing oil to imbue.

Anoint the tent, the ark, and all inside,
The table, the lamp stand, and the altars to provide,
Consecrate them to be most holy,
Aaron and his sons too, to serve solely.

Speak to the sons of Israel and say,
This holy oil shall be used this way,
Not to be poured on anyone's body,
Nor made again in the same quantity.

Spices for incense, stacte and onycha too,
Galbanum and frankincense, a sacred brew,
Beaten and mixed, a fragrant blend,
Sacred to the Lord, it shall ascend.

These are the instructions the Lord gave,
For a place where His presence He'll engrave,
For all His people to follow and serve,
In the way, His glory they deserve.

GIFTED HANDS

From the mouth of the Lord above,
Moses heard His sacred love,
"Bezalel, son of Uri and Hur,
Filled with spirit, wisdom pure.

Craftsmanship in every kind,
In gold and silver he'll design,
Bronze and stone, wood carving too,
All that I command, he'll do.

Oholiab, of Dan's tribe,
Alongside Bezalel will abide,
Skillful hearts with skill I'll fill,
To make the tent, the ark, with will.

The Sabbath day, a sign to keep,
A holy rest, in which to sleep,
Six days of work, but on the seventh,
Complete rest, with God's presence.

Keep it holy, do not profane,
Death to those who work in vain,
For it is a covenant pure,
Between the Lord and Israel sure.

A sign forever, of creation,
Six days of work, then cessation,
On the seventh, the Lord refreshed,
His work complete, His people blessed.

Tablets of stone, written by God's hand,
Given to Moses, on Sinai's land,
A testimony of His love and might,
To guide His people, in truth and light."

SHATTERING THE TABLETS

The people grew restless, as Moses delayed,
From the mountain, they feared he'd been waylaid,
So they approached Aaron with a demand,
"Make us a god," they said, "to lead our band."

Aaron then instructed them to bring
Their golden earrings, for a sacred thing,
From which he crafted a metal calf,
Which they worshiped with a raucous laugh.

When Moses returned, he was filled with ire,
As he saw the people's sinful desire,
He shattered the tablets at his feet,
And made them drink the calf, crushed and beat.

Moses asked Aaron, "Why did you do this?
And bring upon the people such a great abyss?"
But Aaron pleaded with him to be calm,
For the people were prone to evil's charm.

Then Moses called out to the faithful few,
"Join me, and the Lord's work we will pursue."
The sons of Levi heeded his call,
And killed those who worshiped the idol tall.

Moses prayed to the Lord, and He did relent,
From the harm He intended, He did repent,
And Moses descended the mountain once more,
With the tablets of testimony, as before.

LAND OF DREAMS

The Lord spoke to Moses, commanding him to go
And lead the people from Egypt's land below
To the land promised to Abraham and his kin
A land flowing with milk and honey, a heavenly win

An angel shall be sent to guide their way
Driving out enemies, they shall not sway
But the Lord would not go with them, it seems
For they were obstinate and filled with extreme

The people heard this and mourned in sadness
Removing their jewelry in a show of humbleness
For the Lord had warned them of their hard hearts
And the consequences of His presence, tearing them apart

Moses had a tent, a place to meet the Lord
Outside the camp, where seekers could afford
To come and worship, to seek the Almighty's grace
As Moses spoke to the Lord, face to face

Moses asked the Lord to go with them on the way
To distinguish them from others on the earth's sway
For without His presence, they would surely fall
And not find favor, not hear the heavenly call

The Lord promised to go with Moses and his kind
To give them rest and peace, to ease their mind
Moses asked to see the Lord's glory, so grand
But he was only shown His back, not the face so grand.

FRIGHTFUL REVELATION

On Sinai's summit Moses stood,
As God commanded as he should,
With tablets two of stone to hold,
The Lord's commandments to enfold.

No other soul could come that way,
No flocks or herds could come and play,
And there the Lord appeared to he,
In cloud and glory, Moses see.

The Lord spoke words of truth and grace,
Of faithfulness in time and space,
Of mercy, justice, love, and might,
And Moses fell to worship right.

He begged forgiveness for his clan,
And asked that God would hold their hand,
Through wilderness and promised land,
To be their own possession grand.

God made a covenant that day,
And promised mighty works to display,
To drive out foes before their face,
And give them a dwelling place.

The Lord gave laws that they should keep,
To tear down altars, break and sweep,
And never worship other gods,
For jealousy is what He lauds.

Three times a year they'd come to Him,
To worship and confess their sin,
And bring their first fruits to the Lord,
To show they trusted in His Word.

Then Moses wrote the covenant,
And on the tablets it was sent,
And for forty days and nights,
He fasted, prayed, and saw the sights.

As he came down, his face shone bright,
And all who saw were filled with fright,
And yet they knew he'd seen the Lord,
And heard His words, and kept His Word.

BEZALEL'S MASTERWORK

Moses gathered all the sons of Israel,
And spoke the words that God did tell:
"Work six days, but on the seventh rest,
A holy Sabbath, for God's behest.

No fire shall be kindled on this day,
And those who work shall face death's sway.
Bring gold and silver, bronze and more,
Fine linens, skins, and acacia wood galore.

With willing hearts, come make the tent,
And all its coverings, each element.
The ark and poles, the atoning cover,
Table, utensils, and bread to discover.

The lamp stand, the altar, incense too,
Curtains for the doorway, all to ensue.
Bronze grating, basin, hangings, and gate,
Woven garments, for priests to elate.

All who felt stirred or moved inside,
Brought their gifts, with hearts open wide.
Brooches, earrings, bracelets of gold,
And precious stones for beauty untold.

Women spun in colors divine,
While skilled craftsmen worked in line.
Bezalel and Oholiab, filled with grace,
To create and teach, in every place.

God's Spirit filled each one with skill,
To perform His work, with heart and will.
And so the tabernacle was made,
With love and devotion, all fears allayed."

OHOLIAB'S ARTISTRY

Bezalel and Oholiab, skilled by the Lord,
To construct the sanctuary in accord
With His commands, they were called forth to do
And perform all the work, both old and new.

Moses gathered all the skilled in heart
Whose hands were guided by the Lord's impart
They received the gifts the people brought
And continued to bring, their hearts all caught.

The skilled ones said the offerings were enough
For the Lord's construction, so Moses rebuffed
The work to be done was now complete
So the people were restrained from more feats.

The skilled crafted curtains of linen and hues
With cherubim embroidered, work of skilled crews
The curtains were joined and made into sets
With loops and clasps, a structure it begets.

Curtains of goats' hair were made for a tent
Eleven in all, with measurements all bent
The boards were made of acacia wood
Standing upright, as they all should.

Bars of wood were made for each side
Five for each, with a middle bar to abide
The boards overlaid with gold, so bold
And rings of gold, as holders, they hold.

ARK OF THE COVENANT

Bezalel crafted with skill and care,
The ark of acacia wood so rare,
Two and a half cubits long in size,
One and a half in width and height, precise.

Pure gold adorned its interior and out,
A molding of gold, a regal shout,
Four rings of gold on its feet were placed,
Two on each side, securely laced.

Poles of acacia wood overlaid with gold,
Inserted in rings, the ark to hold,
A cover of pure gold, atonement made,
Two and a half cubits long, one and a half wide displayed.

Two golden cherubim he then formed,
At each end, their wings adorned,
Facing each other with wings spread high,
Covering the atoning cover, they comply.

A table of acacia wood he did construct,
Two cubits long, a cubit wide, no defect,
Pure gold overlaid, a molding to surround,
A rim of a hand width, beauty profound.

Four rings of gold on its legs did cling,
Poles of acacia wood with gold, to bring,
Utensils of pure gold, dishes, jars and more,
Fit for a king, a kingly decor.

A lamp stand of pure gold he did make,
Hammered work, cups, bulbs, and flowers to take,
Six branches with almond blossoms, three each side,
Cups and bulbs and flowers, a golden ride.

Four cups shaped like almond blossoms adorned,
Bulbs and flowers, in harmony they formed,
A bulb under each pair of branches, a golden feat,
A single hammered work, pure gold, complete.

The altar of incense of acacia wood so square,
One cubit long, one cubit wide, a two cubit pair,
Horns of one piece, overlaid with pure gold,
A molding of gold, a tale to be told.

Two golden rings, holders for poles he made,
To carry the altar, as commanded, to evade,
Poles of acacia wood with gold, no less,
Holy anointing oil and incense, to bless.

PAT DENIM

A SANCTUARY'S SPLENDOR

In acacia wood, five cubits long,
Five cubits wide, three cubits strong,
The altar of burnt offering stood,
Its corners with bronze horns imbued.

Utensils for the altar, he made,
Of bronze, for sacrifices laid,
Pails, shovels, basins, forks, and pans,
All crafted by skilled artisan's hands.

A grating of bronze beneath it lay,
Reaching halfway up, to hold at bay
The fire's heat, and coals that might spill,
Four rings for poles, made for it to fill.

Poles of acacia, overlaid
With bronze, to be carried in aid,
Inserted in the rings on each side,
A hollow structure to bestride.

A basin of bronze, he then made,
From serving women's mirrors displayed,
Their reflection now a sacrifice,
As water flowed, a symbol of life.

For the courtyard's south side, he wove
Fine linen hangings, a hundred cubits trove,
With twenty pillars, bases, hooks of bronze,
Silver bands, a sight to behold, once.

The north side, same in measure and make,
As the south side, with hooks of silver's stake,
West side, half as long, with ten pillars and bases,
Fifty cubits of fine linen, its graces.

Fifteen cubits of hangings, for each side of the gate,
Three pillars, bases, hooks of silver, to navigate,
Both sides adorned, with their beauty so rare,
A curtain of woven material, its design to bear.

The gate's curtain, twenty cubits in length,
Fine twisted linen, with purple, violet strength,
Scarlet material, to create its display,
Four pillars and bases of bronze, to convey.

All the pegs of the tabernacle and courtyard,
Made of bronze, their strength not to be coward,
The cost of the tabernacle, a great sum,
Counted by Moses, with care and aplomb.

Bezalel, skilled in all that was commanded,
Made everything, with perfection, branded,
Oholiab, an engraver, a weaver so skilled,
Worked with him, to create all that was willed.

Gold, twenty-nine talents, and 730 shekels,
Used in the sanctuary, its design not to wrinkle,
Silver, a hundred talents, and 1,775 shekels too,
Assessed to those counted, to the command, so true.

A beka, half a shekel, for each one above twenty,
603,550 men, in the count aplenty,
One hundred talents for the casting of the bases,
Of the veil, and the hundred bases, for their places.

The hooks for the pillars, their tops overlaid,
With silver bands, for the beauty displayed,
Seventy talents and 2,400 shekels of bronze,
For the altar, bases, and pegs, their tone not to be gone.

Thus, the tabernacle was created,
With skilled hands, with care unabated,
A symbol of God's presence and might,
A sanctuary, for His people, to shine so bright.

ROBES OF PURPLE AND BELLS

A holy place, a sacred space,
A place where God could show His face,
With garments made of purple hue,
As God commanded, so they do.

The ephod, woven fine with gold,
A work of art, both strong and bold,
With shoulder pieces, firmly set,
As Moses had been commanded yet.

Onyx stones, in gold filigree,
Placed on the shoulder, we can see,
To be a reminder of each son,
As God had said, it must be done.

The breastplate, crafted carefully,
With precious stones, arranged to be,
A symbol of the tribes of old,
To represent, in tales retold.

With twisted cords of purest gold,
Chains like cords, that were foretold,
Attached the breastplate to the ephod,
As God had said, so it was showed.

The robe, all violet in hue,
Was crafted with a careful view,
With pomegranates on the hem,
And golden bells, that rang like gems.

The tunics and the linen wear,
Of Aaron and his sons, a pair,
Were made with fine and woven thread,
As God had said, so it was led.

And lastly, on the holy crown,
Inscribed with words of high renown,
The phrase "Holy to the LORD",
As God had said, and all adored.

The tabernacle now complete,
With furnishings, all neat and sweet,
As God had said, the people do,
And bring it to Moses, all anew.

FOLLOWING A CLOUD

The Lord spoke to Moses, so divine,
"On the first day of the month, align
The tabernacle, with utmost care
Place the ark and veil it there

Bring in the table and set it right
And the lamp stand, let there be light
The gold altar of incense, too
In front of the ark, for a holy view

The burnt offering altar, in sight
Before the tent, a holy rite
Between the altar and tent of meeting
Place the basin for washing, and be fleeting

The courtyard, hang up its gate
Set it up all around, don't be late
Anoint everything, make it holy
Furnishings and Aaron, who is solely

To serve as a priest, anointed true
With his sons, who wear tunics new
All consecrated, to serve the Lord
Their anointing, a permanent accord

On the first day of the second year
The tabernacle was erected, clear
Moses laid its bases, set the boards
Inserted bars and pillars, all in one accord

The tent was spread, just as told
Testimony in the ark, poles to hold
The atoning cover placed on top
Veil for the covering, nothing to stop

The table on the north side set
With bread arranged, a holy asset
Lamp stand opposite, on the south side
Lamps lit before the Lord, with pride

Gold altar placed in front of the veil
Incense burned, nothing to fail
The curtain for the doorway set
Burnt offering altar in front, don't forget

The basin between the altar and tent
For washing hands and feet, a good intent
The courtyard hung up its gate
All complete, nothing left to debate

The cloud covered the tent of meeting
Glory of the Lord, a sight so fleeting
Moses unable to enter in
Cloud settled, a new journey begin

Whenever the cloud was taken up high
The Israelites knew it was time to fly
And if the cloud remained in place
They stayed put, no need to race

Throughout their journeys, a constant guide
The cloud of the Lord, never to subside
By day, a cloud, by night, fire bright
In sight of Israel, a holy sight.

BLOOD IS SHED

From the tent of meeting, the LORD called
And to Moses, His words were told
"Speak to Israel's sons," He said
"For offerings to Me, they must be led"

From the herd or flock, their gifts must come
A male without defect, for the burnt offering some
At the doorway of the tent of meeting, it must be laid
So that acceptance before Me can be made

With hands laid on the offering's head
Atonement is made, as blood is shed
Aaron's sons, the priests, then take their place
Sprinkling blood on the altar with grace

The burnt offering is then skinned and cut
The sons of Aaron arrange it, but
First, fire must be set and wood arranged
The pieces placed atop, head and suet exchanged

Entrails and legs are washed with care
Then up in smoke, the offering is aired
A soothing aroma, an offering by fire
To the LORD it's given, His heart's desire

If the offering is from the flock
A male without defect, as before, is sought
Slaughtered northward, its blood is spread
On the altar, where it will be fed

Cut into pieces, with head and suet in tow
Arranged on the fire, the aroma will grow
Entrails and legs, again washed with care
Then up in smoke, the offering they share

And for birds, turtledoves or young doves suffice
Their heads pinched off, their blood drained precise
Craw and feathers removed, thrown to the east
Torn by wings, but not severed, on the wood, they'll feast

Ascending in smoke, the offering's embrace,
Upon the altar, a soothing aroma takes place.
By fire, to the LORD, it's dedicated,
Love, mercy, and grace, in this act orchestrated.

AROMA OF DEVOTION

With reverence, fine flour and oil we'll prepare,
To the priests, with frankincense, a sacred share.
A handful taken, offered on the altar's height,
A memorial, a soothing aroma, pleasing in God's sight.

From the oven, grain offerings shall arise,
Unleavened cakes with oil, a savory prize.
Or wafer, mixed with fine flour, light and pure,
Baked on a griddle, oil poured, an offering sure.

In a pan, fine flour blended with oil so fine,
Presented to the priest, to the altar we align.
In smoke, it ascends, a memorial to revere,
A soothing aroma, God's pleasure it appears.

By fire, leaven and honey shall not be consumed,
For the first fruits, a covenant, salted and perfumed.
Early ripened produce, to the Lord, we bring,
Fresh heads of grain roasted, with fire's embrace we sing.

Crushed grain, new growth, anointed with oil and scent,
In smoke, it shall rise, as a memorial, heaven-sent.
A soothing aroma, pleasing to the divine,
This offering embraced, in God's presence will shine.

OFFERINGS AT THE DOOR

In offerings f peace,
male or female from the herd,
without blemish they must be,
to present before the Lord.

Lay your hands upon its head,
slay it at the tent's door,
blood upon the altar shed,
by Aaron's sons in holy chore.

Present the sacrifice of peace, divine,
Offer the entrails' fat, a sacred sign,
With kidneys and liver, let them be,
A pleasing aroma, the offering's plea.

If from the flock, the offering came,
without defect it must be,
male or female, just the same,
an unblemished lamb or goat to see.

Lay your hands upon its head,
slay it in front of the tent,
then let the blood be sprinkled
as an offering to God sent.

From the sacrifice of peace,
offer up the fat and more,
all the entrails' fatty piece,
a pleasing aroma to adore.

This statute is forevermore,
no fat or blood to be eaten,
an offering to God we pour,
with hearts and hands unbeaten.

GUILT ERASED

If the congregation sins unintentionally,
And the matter goes unnoticed, it's clear to see,
The same as the priest, a bull must be given,
To be offered before the Lord, and sins forgiven.

The elders of the congregation lay hands,
On the bull's head, before the Lord it stands,
Slaughtered, blood taken, sprinkled once again,
On the horns and base of the altar, free from sin.

The fat taken out, on the burnt altar placed,
The bull's offered, and sins are erased,
The priest makes atonement, sins forgotten,
God's grace given, and mercy begotten.

When a leader sins, and guilt is to blame,
A male goat, without defects, is the same,
Laid hand on, slaughtered, blood taken out,
On the burnt altar, sin's hold is devout.

If a commoner sins unintentionally,
By breaking God's law, sinning innocently,
A female goat, without defects, must be brought,
And offered before the Lord, as God has taught.

Laid hand on, slaughtered, blood taken,
On the horns and base of the altar, sin forsaken,
Fat removed, on the burnt altar placed,
Sin's hold broken, and guilt is erased.

So follow God's laws, with all your might,
And if sin comes, bring a sacrifice to the light,
Offer it before the Lord, with a pure heart,
And in His grace and mercy, you'll never depart.

SIN'S PRICE PAID

Confess your sin when you bear witness,
Or face punishment for your fitness.
Touch not unclean things, or you'll be guilty,
Even if they're hidden and filthy.

If you touch human uncleanness,
And later find out in your weakness,
You will be guilty of this offense,
And must confess without defense.

If you swear thoughtlessly with your lips,
And later learn of your sins and slips,
You will be guilty and pay the price,
Confess your wrongdoing, don't think twice.

Bring a female from the flock,
Or a lamb or goat as your sin's stock,
To make atonement for your wrong,
And to show the Lord that you belong.

If you can't afford a lamb to bring,
Two turtledoves or young doves will sing,
One for the sin, one for burnt offering,
The priest will make atonement, forgiving.

If even doves are out of reach,
A tenth of fine flour will be your speech,
A sin offering without oil or spice,
Presented to the Lord, it will suffice.

If you sin against the holy thing,
Bring a ram without defect, it'll sing,
Make restitution and add a fifth,
The priest will make atonement, a gift.

If you sin unknowingly,
A guilt offering will set you free,
Bring a ram without defect to the priest,
Make atonement, and you'll be released.

Whether intentional or not,
If you sin, confess on the spot,
Bring your offering to the Lord,
Make atonement, and be restored

FRAGRANCE OF FORGIVENESS

When the Lord spoke, His words rang true,
Addressing sins and actions askew.
For those who disregard their neighbor's right,
Be it deposit, security, or unjust slight.

If robbery or extortion they commit,
Or found lost goods, deceitfully omit,
False oaths and any form of sin,
Restitution required, guilt to rescind.

Return what's taken with an added share,
Give to the rightful owner, showing care.
Bring a guilt offering, a flawless ram,
To the priest, seek atonement, where shadows dim.

The fire for burnt offerings must never fade,
Priests keep it burning, their duty obeyed.
Garbed in linen, they remove the ash,
Offer the fat portions, a fragrant splash.

Grain offerings presented before the altar grand,
Lifted by Aaron's sons with practiced hand.
Burned as a pleasing aroma, pure and mild,
Priests partake, consuming with reverence styled.

The sin offering, holy and true,
Priests partake in a place reserved, not askew.
Whoever touches its flesh shall be set apart,
Garments washed if blood spatters impart.

These laws from the divine should not be missed,
With each offering, forgiveness shall persist.

THE SIGNIFICANCE OF BLOOD

A law of guilt and sacrifice,
Most holy, to the Lord we raise,
In place of burnt, the guilt shall die,
Blood on altar, sprinkled in praise.

The fat, the tail, and entrails' coat,
Two kidneys with their loins adorn,
The liver's lobe and kidneys smote,
Offered in smoke to God, reborn.

All male priests may partake and eat,
In holy place, most sacred right,
Guilt and sin, one law to meet,
Priest's atonement, shines bright.

To priests, burnt offering's hide is due,
Grain offering's, in oven baked,
And all in pan or griddle too,
To priests presenting, share is staked.

Oil mixed with grain, to Aaron's kin,
Equal for all, to share alike,
Thanksgiving, peace offering win,
Unleavened cakes, and wafers spike.

One of each, offered in turn,
To Lord, contribution be,
The flesh, on day of offering burn,
No leftovers, morning to see.

But vow or voluntary, wait,
Eaten on day, and next to come,
Third day's flesh, by fire's fate,
Unclean, and bear the guilt of some.

Touching unclean, detestable thing,
Eating flesh of peace offering's right,
Cut off from people, you will cling,
And bear the punishment, in God's sight.

No fat from ox, goat or sheep,
No fat from those who die or torn,
Eating such, the price to keep,
Cut off from people, in anger's scorn.

Blood of bird or animal, don't eat,
In any dwellings, be aware,
Eating blood, your life, forfeit,
Your people, forevermore, you'll spare.

Sacrifice of peace, with care,
Bring offering to the Lord,
Fat with breast, to be offered there,
Wave offering, in accord.

Fat on altar, smoke arise,
Breast to Aaron, for his sons,
Right thigh to the priest, in wise,
Allotted portion, from God's sons.

This is the allotment, from the fire,
To Aaron and his sons, forevermore,
On the day they were chosen, to inspire,
Serve the Lord, and His people, adore.

ANOINTING OIL AND BLOOD

The Lord spoke to Moses, His voice clear,
"Take Aaron, his sons, and all they need here,
Garments, anointing oil, the bull for sin,
Two rams, unleavened bread, and then

Assemble the congregation at the tent's door,
This is the commandment, hear it once more."
Moses obeyed, gathered the crowd,
"This is what the Lord wants," he said aloud.

Aaron and his sons came forth to stand,
Moses washed them with water from his hand.
He dressed Aaron in a tunic and sash,
Robe, ephod, and a band with artistic flash,

Then the breastplate and Urim and Thummim,
A holy crown on the turban to finish him.
Next came the anointing oil, consecrating all,
The tabernacle and its contents standing tall,

The altar, its utensils, the basin and stand,
All anointed and pure at God's command.
Moses poured oil on Aaron's head,
Consecrating him as the high priest led,

And then Aaron's sons were clothed the same,
Tunics, sashes, and caps in the Lord's name.
The bull for sin offering was brought forth,
Aaron and sons laid their hands on its worth,

Moses slaughtered it, its blood on the altar spread,
The altar was purified and consecrated.
The fat and liver lobe and kidneys too,
Moses offered in smoke to God's view,

The bull and its hide, flesh, and refuse,
Burned outside the camp as God did choose.
A ram for the burnt offering was presented,
Aaron and his sons laid their hands, contented,

Moses slaughtered it, its blood on the altar flung,
Then the head and suet on the altar were hung.
Moses washed the entrails and legs with water clear,
The whole ram offered in smoke, a soothing aroma dear,

An offering by fire to the Lord, as He decreed,
Moses' obedience and reverence, indeed.
Another ram was brought forth, for ordination,
Aaron and his sons laid their hands with anticipation,

Moses slaughtered it, bloodied Aaron's ear, thumb, toe,
The same for his sons, the blood sprinkled to and fro.
The fat and liver lobe, kidneys, and right thigh,
And unleavened bread from the basket nearby,

Placed on the portions of fat and on the right thigh,
A wave offering before the Lord on high.
Moses took the breast and offered it too,
As a wave offering to the Lord, it was his due,

The ram of ordination, his portion to claim,
Just as the Lord had commanded, no blame.
Anointing oil and blood, sprinkled on all,
Garments and sons consecrated, standing tall,

Moses instructed Aaron and his sons to boil the flesh,
And eat it with bread, an ordination offering afresh.
The people obeyed, as Moses had commanded,
Thus the ordination of Aaron and his sons was branded.

FIRE FROM ABOVE

On the eighth day, Moses called
Aaron and his sons, and elders all
"Take a calf, a bull, without defect
A ram for burnt offering, also select"

"Speak to Israel, take a male goat
And a lamb and a calf, one year old, remote
Without defect, burnt offering to be
An ox and a ram for peace offerings, see?"

So they took what Moses said, obeyed
And before the Lord they all arrayed
"This is the Lord's command," said he
"So His glory may appear and we may see"

Aaron came near to offer his sin
And burnt offering for his kin
He dipped his finger in the blood
And on the altar's horns, he stood

The flesh and hide burned outside the camp
The burnt offering presented, blood and lamp
Aaron washed the entrails and the legs
Offered them up in smoke, no delays

For the people, the goat was slain
Burnt offering, he presented again
The grain offering in his hand
Offered up in smoke as planned

The ox and ram for peace offerings too
Fat portions placed on breasts, no ado
Breasts and thigh presented as wave
And all the people were saved

Aaron blessed them and stepped down
Sin, burnt, peace offerings all were done
Moses and Aaron went into the tent
Blessed the people and His glory was sent

Fire went out from the Lord
Consumed the offerings with His word
The people shouted and fell down
Face to the ground, His glory crowned.

DEVOURED BY FIRE

Two sons of Aaron, Nadab and Abihu,
Offered strange fire, which they were not to do.
From the Lord, a fire came and devoured,
Leaving them lifeless, before Him they cowered.

Moses then spoke to Aaron, his brother,
The Lord's command was clear, like no other.
Carry your brothers away from the place,
Out of the camp, in coats, with solemn grace.

Uncover not your heads, tear not your clothes,
Lest death befall you, as the Lord foreknows.
Let your brethren mourn the burning, it's true,
For the Lord has kindled it, they must pursue.

Stay inside the tabernacle, remain,
The anointing oil upon you must sustain.
They listened to Moses, obeyed his decree,
Abiding within, as the word did decree.

The Lord spoke to Aaron, with instruction,
No wine or strong drink in the holy function.
To discern the holy from the profane,
Teach Israel the statutes, their hearts to train.

Moses then told Aaron and his sons,
Take the remaining offerings, chosen ones,
Eat without leaven beside the altar's grace,
For it is most holy, a divine embrace.

In a clean place, the wave breast and shoulder,
Shall be shared with your daughters, making you bolder.
A perpetual statute, for all to abide,
As the Lord has commanded, let it reside.

Moses searched for the sin offering goat,
But found it burnt, his anger afloat.
Why did you not eat it, as you should?
Aaron explained, and Moses's anger withstood.

DIETARY RESTRICTIONS

The Lord spoke to Moses and Aaron, clear,
To the sons of Israel, these rules adhere:
Animals with split hoofs and chew their meat,
May be eaten, their flesh you may eat.

Unclean are those with a split hoof they lack,
Like the camel, rabbit, and rock hyrax track.
Sea creatures with fins and scales are fine,
Without both, their flesh you must decline.

Detest the eagle, buzzard, and vulture's flight,
Falcon, raven, and owl's silent night.
Of winged insects, those with jointed legs,
May be eaten, avoid the unclean dregs.

Other winged creatures, four-footed kind,
Detestable, their touch leaves uncleanness behind.
Swarming creatures like the mole and mouse,
Touching them brings uncleanness to your house.

If their carcass falls on a wooden thing,
Or on an earthen vessel, the rule shall cling.
Oven or stove, must be smashed and tossed,
But a spring or cistern remains unscathed, not lost.

If carcass falls on seeds to be sown,
Plant them clean, they can be grown.
Water on seeds with carcass laid,
Unclean, don't plant, it's to be obeyed.

Clean and unclean, these rules made clear,
Follow them well, without fear.
For God is holy, His ways are pure,
Obeying Him, we shall endure.

THE UNCLEAN MOTHER

In hushed tones, the Lord spoke to Moses' ear,
Commands for Israel, His words so clear,
When a boy is born, a mother's joy unfurled,
But her purity tarnished in this ancient world.

For seven days, like her time of blood,
She shall be unclean, her life in a flood,
Then on the eighth day, the child to bless,
Through circumcision, immunity they profess.

And for thirty-three days, she must remain,
In seclusion's shelter, her solitude retained,
Avoiding all that's consecrated and pure,
Till her days of purification, steadfast and sure.

Yet if a daughter enters this earthly space,
Her impurity lingers, a lengthened embrace,
For two weeks, her dwelling is her domain,
And sixty-six days, she must atone, bearing shame.

Once her days of cleansing draw to a close,
An offering she brings, love in her throes,
A lamb, a young dove, or a pigeon, all fair,
To the tent's doorway, the priest shall be there.

The burnt offering and sin offering to make,
From the flow of her blood, she seeks to shake,
The priest, in atonement, shall cleanse her plight,
This law for all mothers, a ritual of light.

But if she's too poor to afford a lamb's grace,
Two turtledoves or young doves she must embrace,
One for the burnt offering, the other for sin,
With the priest's atonement, her victory begins.

In whispered echoes, the Lord spoke anew,
To Moses, His servant, the message grew,
When a woman gives birth to a boy, so dear,
She shall be unclean, her joy shadowed, I fear.

ALONE

When swelling, scab, or spot takes hold,
Skin infected, story unfolds.
To the priest, the afflicted shall go,
His sons too, for all must show.

The priest shall look, with discerning eye,
White hair, deep spot, makes a cry.
Leprosy, unclean, isolated be,
A verdict given, a painful decree.

But if the spot is shallow and bright,
Hair intact, no deeper plight,
Seven days of isolation, wait and see,
On the seventh, check again, rash decree.

If the area fades, no further spread,
Clean you are, infection shed.
Wash your clothes, rejoice, it's clear,
No more fear, the end is near.

But if the rash marches on its way,
Spreading to regions, leading astray,
Return to the priest, unclean declared,
Lesson learned, isolation bared.

A white swelling, hair white and new,
Raw flesh exposed, a chronic clue,
Unclean, no isolation, it's known,
Seek attention, let the truth be shown.

If leprosy covers you, head to toe,.
Pronounced clean, the priest will know.
But raw flesh emerges, unclean to glean,
Isolation near, a harrowing scene.

When raw flesh turns white and pure,
Clean you are, a welcomed cure.
A healed boil leaves behind a spot,
Not leprosy's plot, scar's simple dot.

If burn leaves a spot, reddish-white hue,
Hair turns white, deeper it grew,
Unclean, it's not just a dream,
Infection's grip, a troublesome stream.

But if the bright spot dims its light,
No spreading, keeping strength and might,
Seven days or more, in isolation wait,
Check again, clean you'll be, no debate.

If infection claims your head or beard,
Deep and white, the verdict's heard.
Unclean, isolation becomes your fate,
The priest's check, sealing your state.

But if it's skin deep, brightness wanes,
Seven days' isolation, it sustains,
If it disappears, clean you'll be,
Released from affliction, forever free.

FLIGHT OF THE BIRD

The Lord spoke to Moses, His servant,
Saying, "This is the law of the person
With leprosy, on the day of cleansing:
Bring him to the priest outside the camp.

The priest shall inspect and if he finds
That the leprous infection has been healed,
He shall order to take two clean birds,
Cedar wood, scarlet string, and hyssop to wield.

One bird shall be slaughtered over water,
The live bird, with cedar, hyssop, and string,
Shall be dipped in the blood of the other,
Sprinkled on the one to be made clean.

Then the live bird shall be set free
Over the field, where it shall fly away.
The cleansed shall wash, shave, and bathe fully,
After that, he may enter the camp to stay.

On the eighth day, two male lambs, and one ewe,
Fine flour mixed with oil, a log of oil,
Shall be offered before the Lord, anew.
The priest shall present them in a holy coil.

The lamb shall be slaughtered for guilt offering,
With the log of oil, presented as a wave.
Blood on the right ear, toe, and thumb, sprinkling
Oil on the head and body to behave.

The priest shall offer the sin offering,
And the burnt offering, in holy fire.
Thus, atonement for the cleansed's sins,
And he shall be clean, to his heart's desire.

If he is poor, he may bring only one lamb,
Fine flour mixed with oil, a log of oil,
Two turtledoves, two doves within his ramble,
One for sin, the other for a burnt spoil.

The priest shall wave the lamb and the oil
As a guilt offering before the LORD.
Blood on ear, toe, and thumb, anointed in oil,
Offerings for sin and burnt, in one accord.

The priest shall make atonement for the poor,
Cleansing him of his uncleanness.
Thus, all who obey the LORD's laws pure
Shall enter His presence, with holiness.

IN THE FACE OF FLOW

The LORD spoke to Moses and Aaron, plain,
To the people of Israel, this law shall remain:
When a man has a bodily discharge's flow,
His uncleanness is not to be taken slow.

Whether it flows freely or is held within,
His uncleanness shall be treated as a sin.
Every bed he lies on becomes unclean,
Touched by him, impurity is seen.

Anyone who touches his bed or seat,
Must wash their clothes and bathe, complete.
They shall remain unclean until evening,
For his discharge is not a pleasant thing.

Whoever he touches must also wash,
Clothes and bathe to avoid a rash.
If he spits on someone who is clean,
The same ritual shall be routine.

Every saddle he rides upon,
Becomes unclean, defiled and undone.
And anyone who touches what's under him,
Shall be unclean till evening, dim.

If the man with discharge touches another,
The touched one must wash to recover.
Clothes must be cleaned to rid of impurity,
And bathing ensures cleanliness with surety.

Earthenware touched by him shall be broken,
Wooden vessels rinsed, a precaution spoken,
To prevent his uncleanness from spreading,
And keep the purity intact, no dreading.

When the man is cleansed from his discharge's stain,
He shall count seven days, cleanse not in vain,
Wash clothes, bathe in running water's flow,
To become clean, free from filth's shadow.

On the eighth day, he shall come,
Before the LORD, to the tent's sacred drum,
With two turtledoves or young doves in hand,
To make atonement for his discharge, a command.

If a man has a seminal emission's release,
He shall bathe his body, seeking peace,
And remain unclean until evening falls,
His discharge's impurity within walls.

Any garment or leather he touches, too,
Shall be washed and left unclean, no undo.
If he sleeps with a woman and has an emission,
Both shall bathe, ensuring a new mission.

When a woman has a discharge of blood,
For seven days, she's in menstrual impurity's flood.
Whoever touches her shall be unclean till evening,
For her discharge is unclean, no redeeming.

Everything she lies or sits upon,
Shall be unclean, a stain not gone.
And whoever touches her bed or seat,
Shall wash clothes and bathe, a hygiene feat.

If a man sleeps with her, his impurity lasts,
For seven days, his uncleanness casts.
Every bed he lies on shall be unclean,
Until the discharge from her body is seen.

If a woman has a non-menstrual discharge's trace,
Continuing for many days, a different case,
She shall remain in her impure state,
Like her menstrual impurity, it's fate.

Any bed she lies on, unclean it shall be,
And whoever touches her, unclean they'll see.
They must wash clothes and bathe anew,
To cleanse themselves from her impurity's brew.

When she becomes clean from her discharge's plight,
She shall count off seven days, shining bright.
Bring two turtledoves or young doves pure,
To make atonement for her impure allure.

So keep the sons of Israel separated,
From their uncleanness, don't be belated.
Lest they die in their impurity's sorrow,
Defiling the tabernacle, a bleak tomorrow.

This is the law for those with a discharge's flow,
And for those with seminal emission, we know.
And for women ill from menstrual impurity,
And those who sleep with an unclean woman, clarity.

FATE OF THE GOAT

The Lord spoke to Moses on that day,
After Aaron's sons had passed away.
He shared with Moses instructions clear,
Regarding atonement, so all would hear.

Tell Aaron he must not enter in,
Inside the veil, the Holy Place to begin,
Before the atoning cover on the ark's chest,
Or face the consequence, his life put to rest.

Let Aaron bring a bull for sacrifice,
And a ram, a burnt offering precise.
Put on linen tunic and turban clean,
Bathe in water, a symbol of being pristine.

From the congregation, two goats shall be brought,
One for a sin offering, a significant thought.
Cast lots for the Lord, to choose their role,
One for sacrifice, the other for a separate stroll.

Once atonement for himself is made,
Aaron shall enter the tent, unafraid.
With sweet incense and fire in his hand,
Sprinkle the bull's blood on the cover, as planned.

Slaughter the goat for sin offering's sake,
Bring its blood to the cover, a step to take.
Make atonement for impurities and sins,
For the tent and the meeting place it begins.

No one shall be in the tent's domain,
As Aaron makes atonement, a sacred campaign.
Sprinkle the altar's horns with blood applied,
To cleanse it from impurities that hide.

When all is done, present the live goat,
Lay hands on it, confessing Israel's wrongs remote.
Send it away to the wilderness, set it free,
Symbolizing removal of guilt for all to see.

Aaron shall remove his linen attire,
Bathe in holy water, cleanse and aspire.
Put on his regular clothes once more,
Offer burnt and sin offerings as before.

The one who led away the scapegoat shall return,
But the bull and goat for sin offering must burn.
Taken outside the camp, consumed by fire's might,
Their hides, flesh, and refuse vanish from sight.

FORBIDDEN SECRETS

The Lord spoke to Moses, saying:
"Speak to Aaron and his kin,
To all of Israel's sons,
And tell them this commandment I bring:

Anyone who slaughters an ox,
A lamb or goat, inside or out,
But does not bring it to the tent,
To present to the Lord devout,

Bloodshed is counted against them,
Cut off from among their people,
So bring your sacrifices here,
To the doorway of the temple.

The priest shall sprinkle blood on the altar,
Offer up fat as a soothing scent,
No longer worship goat demons,
A permanent statute to prevent.

If anyone offers a sacrifice,
But does not bring it to the Lord,
They too shall be cut off,
Their fate to be forever ignored.

Anyone who eats blood,
Shall be cut off from their kin,
For the life of flesh is in the blood,
The Lord's atonement to begin.

So do not eat the blood of any flesh,
Nor an animal torn by beasts,
Wash your clothes and bathe in water,
To be clean as the law decrees.

For those who do not cleanse themselves,
Will bear the burden of their guilt,
Obey these laws, and you'll remain pure,
By the Lord's commandments, forever built."

FORBIDDEN ACTS

The voice of the Lord spoke out to Moses,
Saying, "Speak to Israel, heed My poses.
I am the Lord, your God, you must obey,
And not follow the heathen's wicked way.

Do not act like Egypt or Canaan's land,
Do not walk in their statutes, understand?
Follow My judgments and keep My decree,
And live in harmony, for I am He.

Observe My statutes and My judgments true,
And whoever follows them will live anew.
Do not uncover a relative's nakedness,
For that is an offense of great likeness.

Your father's wife's nakedness don't reveal,
Nor your daughter's, nor daughter-in-law's deal.
Your brother's wife, don't uncover her shame,
Nor take a woman's sister as a second dame.

During her menstrual impurity,
Do not approach a woman impurely.
Do not sleep with a man like with a mate,
Or with an animal, it's an abominable state.

Do not defile yourselves with these things,
As the nations I drive out were filthy kings.
I'll punish the land that is defiled,
And vomit out its people, so it's exiled.

Keep My statutes and do not defile,
For whoever does so will be cut off from the pile.
Observe your commitment to Me,
And do not practice abominable customs, see?
For I am the Lord, your God indeed."

FAIR JUDGMENTS, JUST MEASURES

The LORD spoke to Moses, so it's told,
And said to all the sons of old,
"Be holy, for I am the Lord,
Revere your parents, keep my word.

My Sabbath days you shall observe,
And idols, cast them to the curb.
Peace offerings must be consumed,
No leftovers shall be assumed.

Oppress not your neighbor or the poor,
Nor curse the deaf, nor close the door
To the blind; judge your neighbor fair,
And slander not, nor cause despair.

Love your neighbor as you do yourself,
Keep My statutes on your shelf.
For three years, fruit shall not be eaten,
On the fourth, it shall be beaten.

Do not practice divination or spells,
Trim not your beard or your locks as well.
No tattoos, nor cuts for the dead,
And Sabbaths and sanctuary you shall tread.

Honor the elders, fear your God,
And treat the stranger as you would the odd.
Keep fair judgment in weight and measure,
For I am the Lord, your holy treasure.

So keep my statutes and ordinances too,
For I am the Lord, who freed you
From the land of Egypt's chains,
And to you, I bring eternal gains."

PURE GIFTS

The Lord spoke to Moses with care,
Giving rules for offerings, a sacred affair.
Aaron and his sons were to take heed,
To ensure the gifts brought were pure indeed.

No unclean man could approach with sin,
Lest they be cut off, God's presence thin.
Even Aaron's descendants with leprosy,
Must be clean before partaking, you see.

Those who touched corpses or had discharge,
Needed cleansing before consuming the message.
Unclean things meant no holy food to eat,
Bathing and cleansing were required to meet.

Animals that died or were torn apart,
Were unclean, unfit for any heart.
Priests had to be faithful, no room for sin,
To consume the holy, for God sanctified them.

Laymen couldn't eat the holy gift,
Only priests and their household could uplift.
If a priest bought a slave, they could partake,
And those born in his house, for God's sake.

A priest's daughter who married a layman,
Couldn't eat the holy ram, according to the plan.
If widowed, she could return and eat again,
But not for others, this rule would remain.

Unintentional eating of holy food,
Required a fifth to the priest, as it should.
The holy gifts must not be profaned,
Punishment for guilt would surely be gained.

Offerings to the Lord, whether vow or choice,
Must be without defect, a perfect voice.
No offering with flaw would be accepted,
Peace offerings too, flaw-free, were expected.

Blind, fractured, or maimed, they couldn't be,
Offerings with deformities were not to see.
The Lord would not accept such a flawed sight,
Perfection was required, with no blight.

An overgrown or stunted flock member,
Could be offered voluntarily, no censor.
But not for a vow, it had no place,
The Lord wouldn't accept it, no trace.

Crushed or torn-off testicles were banned,
No offering or food, they couldn't withstand.
Such flawed things must not be given to the Lord,
For they were unfit, to be in accord.

Newborn animals must stay with their mother,
For seven days before sacrificing, no other.
On the eighth, they could be brought to the altar,
But not the young and mother, it would falter.

Slaughtering both on the same day was wrong,
Thanksgiving offerings had a different song.
Consume it all on that very day,
No storing allowed, no delay.

Keep and do God's commandments, He said,
For He is the Lord, our righteous thread.
His holy name must never be profaned,
For He sanctifies us, forever sustained.

SACRED TIMES

The Lord to Moses spoke, decreeing,
"Mark times divine, hearts believing,
Holy gatherings, hold them dear,
For all the sons of Israel, clear.

Rest on the seventh, Sabbath's embrace,
Convocation holy, no toil's chase,
In every dwelling, declare the decree,
A day of peace, for you and Me.

Appointed times, sacred embrace,
Announce them all, proclaim their grace,
On fourteenth's twilight, Passover's start,
A feast to honor, from the heart.

Feast of Unleavened Bread, so true,
Fifteenth's dawn, seven days through,
A holy convocation, the first day bold,
Offerings rise, stories to be told.

As harvest's bounty, your hands bring,
First fruits to the priest, a sacred thing,
Wave before Me, acceptance's sign,
On Sabbath's morrow, let them shine.

With a lamb, one year, pure and fine,
Two-tenths of oil and flour align,
A fourth of wine, fragrance and fire,
An offering pleasing, rising higher.

Count seven Sabbaths, days to count,
From Sabbath's end, new offering's mount,
Fifty days pass, a grain's fresh bread,
Two loaves with leaven, joy widespread.

Seven male lambs, a bull, rams in sight,
A goat for sin, peace's lamb alight,
Wave with first fruits, a joyful blend,
Convocation holy, hearts on mend.

When harvest's riches, your hands shall hold,
Leave for the needy, stories unfold,
Strangers too, care they find,
I, the Lord, in all mankind.

Seventh month's first, the trumpet's call,
A holy pause, a rest for all,
Convocation's fire, offerings rise,
A sacred day, under open skies.

Tenth day humbles, atonement's plea,
No labor done, hearts set free,
Lest separation, you face alone,
A holy gathering, humbly shown.

Fifteenth's glory, Booths arise,
Seven days to joy, under open skies,
Convocation pure, hearts full of cheer,
Offerings lifted, a festive sphere.

Appointed times, a statute kept,
Generations pass, no memory swept,
In dwelling places, near and wide,
Convocations holy, in love they bide."

CURSING GOD'S NAME

Oil from beaten olives, clear and pure,
Commanded by the Lord to procure,
To make a lamp burn day and night,
Before Him in the tent of light.

Aaron must keep it in order and right,
From evening till morning, it's his sight,
A statute forever, for generations to come,
The lampstand of gold, for all to see some.

Twelve cakes of fine flour, baked to perfection,
Two-tenths of an ephah in each section,
Set in two rows on the table of gold,
With pure frankincense, a sight to behold.

Every Sabbath day, set in order with care,
Before the Lord, a covenant to bear,
An offering by fire, a memorial of bread,
For the sons of Israel, an everlasting thread.

But if anyone curses God's holy name,
He will bear the burden of his sin and shame,
And if anyone takes a human life,
He must be put to death, that's the strife.

An animal's life can be repaid,
Life for life, restitution made,
Injury for injury, tooth for tooth,
Inflicted upon the offender, that's the truth.

Whether native or stranger, one standard for all,
For the Lord is God, He'll hear the call,
So the sons of Israel did just as He commanded,
Stoning the blasphemer, justice demanded.

FAIR TRANSACTIONS

The Lord spoke from Mount Sinai,
To Moses, saying, "Listen well,
When you reach the land I'll give,
The Sabbath's law I shall tell.

For six long years, your fields will grow,
You'll reap your harvests, oh so fine,
But in the seventh year, you'll know,
Your land shall rest, it shall be mine.

The seventh year will be a time,
A Sabbath to the Lord of all,
No sowing, pruning, or reaping chime,
You shall not plant, nor shall you haul.

The land will have a sabbatical,
No reaping grapes, nor aftergrowth,
A time of rest, both big and small,
To give the earth a chance to grow.

All shall share in the land's produce,
The Sabbath year will bring forth food,
For those who live there, what's the use,
You'll eat your fill, and none will feud.

For forty-nine years, you will count,
Seven Sabbaths of years, they'll be,
The fiftieth year will be a mount,
Of jubilee for you and me.

On the tenth day of the seventh month,
A ram's horn will sound through the land,
On the Day of Atonement, a holy front,
A time of release and a new stand.

The fiftieth year will be a time,
Of jubilee, you'll sow no seed,
Nor will you harvest grapes or climb,
To prune the vines, or do the deed.

The fiftieth year will be holy,
Eat from the field, its produce fine,
All shall return to what's solely,
Theirs and their family's line.

If you sell to a friend or buy,
Make sure you're fair, and do no wrong,
The years since the last jubilee, apply,
To set the price, it's where we belong.

Do not wrong one another,
But fear the Lord, our God and king,
Follow my statutes, my brother,
My judgments keep, and let them ring.

If you ask, "What will we eat,
In the seventh year, if we don't sow?"
I'll bless your crops in the sixth, and treat,
You well, with enough to help you grow.

If someone sells his property,
He has the right to redeem it back,
Or if he can't, then wait to see,
The year of Jubilee, it's not a lack.

The land is mine, so don't sell it,
For you're just strangers passing by,
If you're poor, and you can't quit,
Your land will stay, you'll not comply.

If someone sells his house in town,
In a year, he can buy it back,
But if he doesn't, he'll have to frown,
The house will pass, it's just a fact.

But villages will have their right,
To buy their land back in Jubilee,
Their fields are open, clear, and bright,
They'll be theirs again, just wait and see.

The cities of the Levites, I'll tell,
Their houses are a possession true,
They can redeem what they sell,
In Jubilee, it'll come back anew.

The pasture fields of Levites' cities,
Can't be sold, for they'll forever be,
A home to cattle, sheep, and kitties,
A place of peace, for all to see."

EXILE AND DESPAIR

Do not make idols or carved images,
Nor bow to stones, nor worship false guises.
Observe my Sabbaths, revere my sanctuary,
For I am the Lord, your God, you shall see.

Follow my statutes, obey my command,
And I'll bless you with rain and fertile land.
The earth will yield produce in its season,
You'll eat in plenty, without rhyme or reason.

By the sword, your enemies shall be slain,
In the land, I'll grant peace, remove all pain.
Harmful creatures, I'll drive them away,
No sword shall harm you, my power will stay.

Among you, I'll dwell, your God, your guide,
From Egypt's bondage, I set you aside.
I broke your yoke, made you stand tall and proud,
In me, your refuge, your voice ever loud.

But if you reject my statutes and ways,
Punishment will come, in distress you'll stay.
Disease, fever, terror shall befall,
Your enemies shall devour what you've sown all

I'll turn against you, your foes will prevail,
The sky like iron, the earth hard as shale.
Your strength will falter, your power decline,
In submission, you'll find no solace, no sign.

If you persist in your hostility,
The plague upon you will multiply, times three.
Your children, taken by beasts of the wild,
Your numbers reduced, your roads left defiled.

And if you still show defiance and hate,
I'll strike you again, a harsher fate.
You'll eat your own children in desperation,
Your sanctuaries desolate, cities in ruin, desolation.

The land will lie barren, observing its rest,
While you suffer in exile, feeling oppressed.
Those who remain will despair in their hearts,
Even the sound of a leaf will tear them apart.

JUST COMPENSATION

Moses was commanded by God,
rules of assessment to applaud,
when making vows, you must be just,
valued according to your trust.

For a male, aged twenty to sixty,
fifty shekels, silver and pretty,
and for a female, thirty would do,
as your assessment, should be true.

If between five and twenty years,
for a male, twenty shekels clears,
and for a female, ten shekels bright,
as your assessment, should be right.

For those under five, a lower fee,
five shekels for males, three for she,
but for sixty-year-olds and above,
assessment, fifteen shekels for love.

If someone's vow cannot be met,
present before the priest, I bet,
the priest will then assess your fate,
according to your means, he'll rate.

If an animal is your vow,
to the Lord, you'll need to endow,
if a clean beast, holy it stays,
but unclean ones, the priest appraise.

Consecrate your house or field,
and the priest shall make it sealed,
as either good or bad, he'll mark,
and as assessed, it will embark.

If you want to redeem the lot,
pay the price and add a fifth to plot,
and if sold, it may not return,
to whom it's owed, it will not adjourn.

The firstborn animal's not yours,
the Lord's property it ensures,
but if unclean, you can redeem,
and add a fifth, as it may seem.

If it's set apart for destruction,
don't sell or buy, it's no induction,
to be destroyed, it's all for God,
it's holy, and that's the nod.

Every tenth part of herd or flock,
is holy to the Lord, no mock,
and for the tithe, it's all for Him,
and if redeemed, add a fifth, slim.

The Lord's rules of valuation,
ensure just compensation,
in all your assessments be fair,
God's holy ways, we must all bear.

OFFERING BY FIRE

On the first day, a convocation holy,
No work to do, only praises solely,
For seven days, offerings by fire to give,
On the seventh day, a convocation to live.

When you enter the land I give to thee,
And harvest its fruits for all to see,
Bring the sheaf of the first fruits to the priest,
Wave it before me, and be pleased.

Count for yourselves, from the day after the Sabbath,
Seven complete Sabbaths, do the math,
Count fifty days until the seventh Sabbath,
Give grain offerings, with bread and wine to have.

Bring two loaves of bread as a wave offering,
With lambs, a bull, and a goat for offering,
Wave them before the Lord, they are holy,
A proclamation to make, a day so holy.

When you reap the harvest, don't forget,
Leave some for the needy, don't regret,
Leave some for the stranger, too,
I am the Lord your God, this I want from you.

In the seventh month, on the first day,
A reminder by blowing trumpets to pray,
A holy convocation, a day of rest,
An offering by fire, to give your best.

On the tenth day, the Day of Atonement,
A holy convocation, a moment,
To humble yourselves and give offerings by fire,
No work allowed, only praise to inspire.

If one doesn't humble on this day so pure,
They shall be cut off, that's for sure,
No work to do, a permanent statute to uphold,
A Sabbath of complete rest, a day so bold.

On the fifteenth of the seventh month, a Feast of Booths,
For seven days, to celebrate the Lord's truths,
The first day, a holy convocation,
No work to do, only praise and adoration.

APPOINTED TIMES

The Lord spoke to Moses, saying,
"Proclaim my appointed times,
Holy convocations, these are they,
For all the sons of Israel to keep.

On the seventh day, rest complete,
A Sabbath, a holy convocation,
No work to be done, for the Lord,
In all your dwellings, this must be.

These are the appointed times,
Holy convocations to proclaim,
In the first month, on the fourteenth day,
At twilight, the Lord's Passover.

And the fifteenth, the Feast of Unleavened Bread,
For seven days, eat unleavened bread,
On the first day, a holy convocation,
Offerings to be made, for seven days.

When you gather the harvest,
Bring the sheaf of first fruits to the priest,
Wave it before the Lord for acceptance,
On the day after Sabbath, wave it.

Offer a male lamb, one year old,
With two-tenths of fine flour and oil,
And a fourth of wine, an offering by fire,
A soothing aroma to the Lord.

Count seven Sabbaths, from the day after Sabbath,
To the fiftieth day, present a new grain offering,
Two loaves of bread, baked with leaven,
Seven male lambs, a bull of the herd, and two rams.

A sin offering of one male goat,
Two male lambs for peace offerings,
To be waved with the bread of first fruits,
A holy convocation, no work to be done.

When you reap the harvest,
Leave the edges and gleaning for the needy,
For the stranger, I am the Lord your God.

In the seventh month, on the first of the month,
A rest, a reminder by blowing of trumpets,
A holy convocation, no work to be done,
Offerings by fire to the Lord to present.

On the tenth day, the Day of Atonement,
A holy convocation, humble yourselves,
No work to be done, make atonement,
Lest you be cut off from your people.

On the fifteenth of the seventh month,
The Feast of Booths, for seven days to the Lord,
A holy convocation, no work to be done,
Offerings to be made, a joyous celebration.

These are the appointed times,
Holy convocations, a permanent statute,
Throughout your generations,
In all your dwelling places, to be kept."

FORGOTTEN INHERITANCE

On Mount Sinai, the Lord spoke to Moses,
Commanding him to relay to the people of Israel
The observance of the Sabbath year,
When the land must rest, untouched by human hand.

For six years, they shall work the land,
Cultivate vineyards, and gather crops with care,
But on the seventh year, a sacred rest,
Dedicated to the Lord, must be observed.

No reaping of after-growth or gathering of grapes,
For the land shall enjoy a sabbatical pause,
And its produce shall be shared by all,
Including the beasts of the field, partaking equally.

Count seven cycles of seven years,
Forty-nine in total for the complete count,
And on the fiftieth year, the jubilee shall sound,
A time of release and liberation across the land.

Each person shall return to their ancestral property,
Reuniting with their families, embracing their roots.
No sowing, harvesting, or grape-picking shall occur,
As the jubilee calls for a holy celebration.

Let no one oppress or take advantage of another,
But fear the Lord and follow His commands,
For the land is sacred, its fruits a blessing,
To be enjoyed by all who uphold His statutes.

The land shall not be sold permanently,
For it belongs to the Lord, not to man.
In every sale, a redemption must be provided,
Restoring the land to its original owner.

If a fellow countryman falls into poverty,
His close relative may redeem his land.
Or if he regains his wealth, he shall repay
The amount to the one who made the purchase.

If he cannot repay, the land remains
In the hands of the purchaser until the jubilee.
And if a house is sold within a walled city,
Redemption rights extend for one full year.

However, if the house is not redeemed in time,
It permanently belongs to the purchaser.
Yet in villages, houses have redemption rights,
And in the jubilee, they shall be restored.

The Levites hold permanent redemption rights
For the houses within their possession.
Their cities' houses are their inheritance,
And they may redeem what rightfully belongs to them.

But the pasture fields surrounding their cities
Shall not be sold, for they belong to the Lord.

Also in the
Threads of Revelation Series:

Destiny's Dance:
Footprints In The Wilderness

Dawn Of Eternity:
Edens Legacy Unraveled

Hi. I hope you have enjoyed this book. If you have a moment to spare, I would greatly appreciate it if you could take the time to review it.

If you gained valuable insights, or if your spiritual journey was influenced in any way, I would love to hear about it. Your opinion matters to me and I would be grateful if you could share your experience and thoughts by leaving a review.

www.ingramcontent.com/pod-product-compliance
Lightning Source LLC
Chambersburg PA
CBHW072008040426
42447CB00009B/1541